Printed in the United States of America

Table of Contents

Introduction

Congratulations on your decision to pursue a teaching career! Teaching can be one of the most rewarding career paths out there. You'll have the opportunity to share your knowledge with and encourage the intellectual growth of young students from all walks of life. And getting your certification through FTCE is a great way to start your career.

Regardless of whether you are still in the process of obtaining your bachelor's degree or if you have multiple years of teaching experience, you've likely been told that you must sit for the FTCE (Florida Teacher Certification Examination) exam. There, you will be required to answer questions that demonstrate your proficiency in your subject area; and you will also need to show that you are competent as an entry-level teaching professional.

We're sure you have questions – everybody does. "How hard is the exam?" "Can I pass on my first try?" "What if I don't? Can I take it again?" "What is even *on* the test?"

Don't worry! We have the answers to all of these questions and more.

While the exam isn't easy, proper planning and preparation can help ensure your success. Sure, you can take the exam again if you fail; but our goal is to give you the keys to outsmarting the exam – the first time around. These first few pages will detail everything you'll need to know about the exam, before leading you into the review material. So get ready to take some notes. Pace yourself. And above all, remember that you are taking the right first step in furthering your career.

Getting to Know the Exam

The Florida Teacher Certification Examinations are developed and administered by the Florida Department of Education. All teaching candidates in the state of Florida are required to pass a general knowledge test, and then an additional exam over their chosen subject matter and grade level.

You don't have to be in the state of Florida to sit for the FTCE exam. A computer-based test, this exam is administered at Pearson VUE testing centers across the world. Pearson is the world's leading testing center network. With over 5,000 testing centers in 175 countries, you can take the exam most anywhere!

Eligibility

If you are still a student at a Florida university finishing your degree or participating in an alternative certification program, you will need to apply for a temporary teaching certificate. In the process of applying for the temporary certificate, you'll be asked which subject matter and grades you are seeking to teach.

The Florida Bureau of Educator Certification will review your eligibility for the FTCE exams. You will receive an Official Statement of Status Eligibility that lists certification exams for which you are eligible. Once you pass each certification exam listed on your Official Statement of Status Eligibility, you may be granted your professional teaching certification for the state of Florida.

If you currently have a professional certification in another state, you can also apply to a temporary teaching certificate in Florida in an effort to be deemed eligible for the test.

To request an Official Statement of Status Eligibility, visit the Florida Department of Education website at www.fldoe.org.

Note: Students or those currently teaching in other states may be required to undergo the FTCE General Knowledge test before sitting for any specialized subject exams.

Important Information: Registration

Once you have been determined eligible to test, you will register for your exam via the FTCE/FELE website (www.fl.nesinc.com). Click the "Register" tab on the website and follow the on-screen prompts. If you do not have a FTCE/FELE account you will need to create one before registering.

Important Information: Fees

You will be assessed a fee of $200 when you register for the exam. In the event that you are unsuccessful in your first bid to pass the exam, you will be charged $220 for each retake.

There are no definite test dates or deadlines to worry about with this exam. You can schedule an appointment year-round to sit for the test. And, as expensive as the actual exam is, at least there are no late registration fees!

What's on the Exam

You'll have 2.5 hours to complete 120 multiple choice questions. The questions will cover the following content:

- The Process of Science
- Science, Technology, and Society
- Chemical Processes of Living Things
- Interactions between cell structure and cell function
- Genetics & Evolution
- Diversity and Function of Life (Plants, Animals, and Organisms)
- Ecology

How is the Exam Scored?

The FTCE will be graded using a scaled score report. You must have at least a **200** to pass the exam.

You will receive notice of your unofficial test results at the testing center when you complete your exam. You will be notified of a "Pass" or "Not Pass" at the testing center. Official test results will be posted online in your FTCE/FELE approximately four weeks following your testing date. Results are typically uploaded by 10:00 PM EST on Tuesdays. You'll receive an email after your exam letting you know when you should start looking for your official results on the FTCE/FELE site.

Test Day

Identification
You will be expected to show a **primary** form of identification at the testing center. In the event that there is any question regarding the validity of the primary identification, secondary identification may be requested. Bring both, just in case.

All forms of identification must adhere to the following criteria:

- **Be Original**: Photocopies are not acceptable.
- **Be Valid**: Expired documents are not acceptable.
- **Bear Full Name EXACTLY as Printed on Admission Ticket**.
- **Bear a Recent Photograph**.
- **Bear Signature of the Individual**.
- **Be Government-Issued**
- **Bear Your Signature**

Examples of **Primary Identification**:

1. Passport.
2. State or Providence ID (including driver's license).
3. Military ID Card.
4. National ID Card.

Examples of **Secondary Identification**:

1. A Second Form of Primary ID.
2. Government-issued ID Card.
3. Student ID Card.
4. Letter from School Confirming Your Identity.

The letter must meet the ID criteria listed above, AND be on school letterhead, AND include a date of issuance, AND bear the signature of a school official, AND bear the official school seal. The signature of a school official and the school seal must overlap your photo on the letter.

Don't Forget Your Admission Ticket!
The Admission Ticket will be emailed to you after you have registered for the exam. You will need to print out the email and bring this with you to the examination.

The name on your Admission Ticket must match the name on your ID. If the two names do not match, you will need to bring documented proof of why the names are different. The documents must be original (no photocopies). Examples of acceptable proof of name change include: Court Order for Name Change; Marriage Certificate; Divorce Certificate; and/or Certification of Naturalization.

You MUST Bring
As you head to the testing center, don't forget to bring your ID and any necessary documentation, as well as your Admission Ticket.

You May Bring
In the event that you have any health-needs related equipment, you will want to obtain approval for this before your testing date. Your health issue must be documented. Submit a request for accommodations, along with supporting documentation, at the time you register for the exam.

You May NOT Bring
Basically, if it's not your Admission Ticket, ID, or any approved device, you can't have it with you. Specifically, you can't bring these items into the testing room: Cell phones, smartphones, or PDAs; any electronic recording, photographic, or listening device; food, drink, or tobacco products; personal items (purses, backpacks, etc.); paper, pencils, notes, reference material, etc.; and/or weapons of any type.

After the Exam

Once you have completed your exam you'll know immediately how well you performed. An <u>unofficial</u> result will be provided at the testing center. Your result will either say "Pass" or "Not Pass."

Official results will be posted to your FTCE/FELE account approximately four weeks after your exam date. Look for results to be published online by 10:00 PM Eastern time on a Tuesday. You will be emailed when your official results are available. Remember, a scaled score of at least 200 is necessary to pass the exam. The test scores remain available online for a period of 60 days.

You will only receive a numeric score if you do not pass the exam. Numeric scores below 200 are offered so that those who seek to retake the exam will know have a better idea of how much additional preparation is needed before retesting. Should you need to retest, remember that you must wait at least 31 days between test sessions.

Scores over 200 are not reported so that the score on the exam cannot be used by school administrators when making a hiring determination between candidates.

If you requested to have your scores automatically sent to any public schools or universities during registration, you will not be required to forward your scores manually. If you did not choose this option, or if you would like to send your score results to additional institutions, you will be responsible for furnishing your own score report and sending the information.

Once you have successfully passed the exam, you will be one step closer to obtaining your professional teaching certification in Florida or to achieving your goal of teaching additional subject matter. The job outlook for middle school teachers is expected to increase faster than average for all occupations, while high school teachers can expect an average rate of job increase in the coming years.

Our goal is to make sure that you pass the exam on your first try. After all, why waste time and money when you can get it right the first time? With that in mind – it's time to begin your review. The concepts which we're about to cover can be very intensive. Make sure to pace yourself, keep separate notes, and – above all – do your best!

Chapter 1: Basic Principles of Science

Scientific inquiry and processes are the backbone of teaching science. These skills hardly ever change, and will carry on with a student throughout all of their science courses. It is important that you the teacher feel comfortable in these areas, as you will be utilizing them every day in the classroom.

Learning and the Ethics of Science

Safety is extremely important while working in the lab. Constant observation of your students is absolutely essential during lab work.

Lab Rules
Always make sure that every person involved in lab activities is familiar with all **lab rules**. A current set of lab rules can usually be found at the beginning of your lab workbook or teacher's manual. The first day of class should consist of a review, and then a quiz, of these lab rules. Students should not work in lab activities until they demonstrate a complete understanding and compliance with these rules.

Materiel Data Safety Sheets (**MSDS**) are used to determine safety concerns and procedures that must be followed when using certain chemicals. Make sure you know the location of all safety equipment in the lab area (e.g. eye wash station, fire extinguisher, safety blanket, etc.) and how to use them.

Safety Hazards
When working in either the lab or the field, constantly look for possible **safety hazards**. Proper safety and first aid training will teach you the proper way to apply such knowledge in an appropriate situation.

Respond to accidents immediately, and make sure students are aware of the procedures they should follow if an emergency or accident occurs.

When performing an activity, make sure you are aware of all **safety rules** and regulations that should be followed during the implementation of the activity. This not only includes safety guidelines to follow but also **safety equipment** that might need to be worn (e.g. safety glasses, apron, etc.). The teacher must also utilize such safety equipment if the activity calls for it.

> While planning, always keep safety in mind. During the development of an activity make sure to think of how accidents can be prevented. These preventions become the safety rules for that activity.

Materials
There are many materials which will be used in the lab with many different purposes: tools, chemicals, specimens, information-gathering devices, etc.

All materials used during an activity including chemicals, tools, equipment, and specimens have safety precautions in order to prevent accidents while using them. It is very important to understand these precautions before using these materials. Also, prevent accidents by knowing how to use the tools and equipment properly.

When handling live organisms, make sure to use proper **ethics** and treatment – this includes a respect for the organism, which ought to be communicated to the entire class. Use **proper disposal** when you are finished using materials. Be **conservative** of the quantities you use and reuse materials when applicable.
Various items can be used to **gather information** during an activity. Calculators, for example, help perform any mathematical computations during the activity. There are three basic types of calculators: four-function, scientific, and graphing.

Another information-gathering device – one which many of your students will well-familiar with – is the **Internet**. The Internet can assist with the collection of background information; performing a quality engine search can often provide all the information you need.

When instructing your students on the proper use of the Internet, make sure to be very clear in your facility's standards of citations.

Many tools, such as **spreadsheets**, **charts**, **tables**, and **graphs**, can be used to display data. Graphs and/or charts will most likely be a part of any activity in which data is collected. **Diagrams**, **maps**, and **satellite images** can be used to show models from the activity. **Written reports** and **oral presentations** are effective ways to communicate results to peers or the general public.

Before using any equipment, make sure it is calibrated. **Calibration** ensures the data output is accurate and precise. With devices that give numerical data (e.g. calculators), you must be certain that the number of significant figures is correct. **Significant figures** refer to the digits that are known with a great deal of certainty.

General rules for significant figures:

- All non-zero numbers are always significant.
- All zero's that are between two non-zero numbers are significant.
- Zero's within a number greater than 10 are significant. If a zero's main purpose is to locate the decimal, it is not significant.

Often during an investigation, you may need access to the natural world. (Studying the growth of plants in certain environments, for example, requires the use of that same environment.) However, in some cases, the natural world is not always accessible; therefore a **model** must be used.

Determining the limitations of a model is an important part of an investigation which helps predict possible error. Perhaps the model is not **physically** correct, and it is either missing parts or requires additional parts. The model might not be **conceptual**, not covering adequately all the bases of the experiment. A **mathematical** limitation could develop as well, where the parts of the model may not fit into proper scale.

Statistical Measures

Though this typically only applies to experimental activities, there are different techniques and technologies that you can use to perform **statistical** measures and analyze the data. The following chart briefly summarizes some statistical tests. Analyze each situation to see when to best use a certain method – most likely, more than one method will be used at a time.

By utilizing the correct way to perform statistical measures, you increase the efficiency of the procedure, as well as its ease and accuracy.

Name of Statistical Method	Example(s)	When to Use
Graphing	Scatter plot, bar graphs, etc.	When comparing measurements
Descriptive Statistics	Mean, median, mode, SD, etc.	When summarizing measurements taken in an activity
Association Statistics	Linear regression	When trying to observe a correlation or regression between variables
Comparative Statistics	t-test and ANOVA	When comparing two or more sets of data
Frequency Statistics	X^2 -test of association	When counts are taken instead of measurements

The **International System of Units** (i.e., metric system) is the universal system of measurement that is utilized in the sciences. The chart below depicts the base units used in science.

Quantity	**Base Unit**
Length	Meter (m)
Mass	Gram (g)*
Temperature	Kelvin (K)
Time	Second (s)

**Although gram is the base unit, kilogram is the most common unit used for mass.*

Conversions for length and mass are simple with the metric system. Prefixes are used to stand for different amounts. The base unit alone is worth 1. To convert, simply divide the base unit by the corresponding amount based on the prefix. The basic prefixes are in the chart below:

Prefix	Amount
Mega (M-)	1 Million
Kilo- (K-)	1 Thousand
Hecto- (H-)	1 Hundred
Deka- (Da-)	1 Ten
Deci- (d-)	1 Tenth
Centi- (c-)	1 Hundredth
Milli – (m-)	1 Thousandth
Micro – (μ-)	1 Millionth

The Nature of Science

Science is the act of studying the physical and natural aspects of the world around us for more understanding. The interaction of science, math, and technology leads to many discoveries about the things that exist in our universe. Science allows us to not only understand our world, but also to make predictions about what is going to happen in our world.

Though science can help us to answer many questions, there are some **limitations** to science, such as **pseudosciences** which deal with the supernatural. For example, you cannot scientifically quantify astronomy and zodiacs (though scientific principles such as consistent measurements and graphs are often used). Science is also of no assistance in the areas of morals and values. It cannot tell us what is good versus bad or how pretty a color is.

> Science is limited to answering questions about the natural world. Science can answer the who, what, when, where, and why of the natural world. It can tell you how old an artifact is or who committed a crime. Science cannot answer questions of opinion or about emotion.

Scientific Investigations

Although limited, science does provide us a means to answering many questions about our natural world. Scientists use different types of investigations, each providing different types of results, based upon what they are trying to find. There are three main types of scientific investigations: descriptive, experimental, and comparative.

Descriptive Investigations

These types of investigations start by making observations. A model is then constructed to provide a visual of what was seen: a *description*. Descriptive investigations do not generally require hypotheses, as they usually attempt to find more information about a relatively unknown topic.

Experimental Investigations

These types of investigations are also referred to as **controlled** experiments because they are performed in a controlled environment. During experimental investigations, all variables are controlled except for one: the dependent variable, which will be the outcome of the experiment. Often, there are many tests involved in this process.

Comparative Investigations

These investigations involve manipulating different groups in order to compare them with each other. There is no control during comparative investigations. Once the investigations are complete, the data is thoroughly analyzed to check for the results or outcome of the manipulated variable.

In order to choose the appropriate type of investigation, scientists must first understand what type of outcome they require. To do this, background information about the topic or question must be collected. The **scientific method** can be used to design an **inquiry-based experiment**. Once that experiment is complete, scientists may communicate their results by writing scientific papers or reports or they participate in scientific presentations or conferences. During the communication phase, whether orally or verbally, scientists have a main goal of defending their points. This defense is built heavily around, not only the procedure and results of the investigation, but also the background research that was performed before the investigation began.

A theory and a hypothesis are both important aspects of science. There is a common misconception that they are one in the same, which is not true – though the two are very similar. A **hypothesis** is based upon background information and research, while a **theory** is formed based on the results of a tested hypothesis.

While testing a hypothesis by way of an investigation, observations are made and data is collected. When a scientist analyzes the data, they are looking for patterns that depict a relationship. If a test is performed multiple times with the same results, concepts can be explained and proven.

The Scientific Method

1. Observe and Ask Questions
2. Research, Collect, and Analyze Data
3. Construct Hypothesis
4. Experiment! Test your Hypothesis
5. Analyze Results and Draw Conclusions
    - Was your Hypothesis True? Report your Results!

- Was your Hypothesis False? Return to Step 3 and Start Again!

Once a scientist has completed and published their scientific paper or presentation, the information must be validated by the science community.

The first step would be to check for logical understanding of the investigation. The entire investigation must make sense before moving on to any other validation points.

The investigation is then peer reviewed. In many cases, this process refers to members of the scientific community performing the investigation again only using the information and procedures provided in the report.

The goal is to get the same results as the original investigator. This is why it is of the utmost importance that the original scientific paper or report be extremely detailed and thorough. Once these processes are complete, the information generated through the investigation is classified as new knowledge.

If the results obtained or not the results expected, there might have been **error** somewhere in the investigation. Errors are common in scientific findings – and so you must always be watchful for them. However, sometimes they are difficult to find. The following steps should be followed when searching for the source of an error.

1. **Repeat** the investigation. Make sure to carefully follow the procedure accurately. In order for information to be validated, it must be repeated numerous times with the same results.

2. If the first step has been followed and there is still error, check the **calibration** of the measuring instruments. When tools aren't properly calibrated, they can't give reliable results.

3. If the tools have been properly calibrated, the **procedure** itself should be thoroughly **examined**. There could be an error in one or more of the steps followed during the investigation.

4. If the tools are calibrated and the procedure is concrete, then perhaps there are **environmental conditions** that should be controlled. Whether an investigation is performed in a lab or in the field, there could be extenuating circumstances that can make for some error in results.
5. Perhaps there is no error in any part of the investigation. The error could lie in how the results were **analyzed**. There could be many ways in which to analyze the results of an investigation. All explanations must be considered.

Systems

A **system** is a whole unit with a main goal, or focus, to work toward; and the system's functions are based on the parts that make up the unit. Take the Respiratory System, for example. It's made up of many functions that all work towards effective respiration.

Each part of a system is interdependent and works together on a common task. All systems have three basic commonalities: structure, action, and interconnectivity.

Structure
All systems have a structure on which the foundation of the system is built. Systems in science have their own unique structure that serves as the systems' base.

Action
All systems perform actions. These actions consist of taking in information, internalizing it, and then giving some type of output.

Interconnectivity
The structures inside of a system all work together so that the system can meet its goals.

Systems can also work with other systems to perform an even bigger goal. The human body is an example of many systems working together for the common goal of keeping the body in equilibrium.

Systems are a part of all the science disciplines, and follow the same basic **model of systems**.

Interacting Parts
The body systems clearly illustrate how systems have interacting parts. Each system contains organs that cooperate in order to keep the whole system functioning.

Boundaries
There is a limit to what a system can do on its own without needing help from other systems. For example, the Earth is a part of the Solar System. The Earth is capable of spinning on its own axis; and this spinning is partly responsible for causing day, night, and season changes. But without the Sun, these processes would not be possible.

Input and **Output**
Systems must receive information in order to send out information. The input could be in the form of instructions, like when the nucleus of a cell gives instructions to the other organelles on when and what function they should be performing.

Feedback
Feedback occurs when a portion of the output is returned to the system and used to control or maintain the system. Nature, for instance, is constantly recycling itself in a great example of feedback.

Subsystems

Sometimes larger systems are made of smaller, independent systems. For example, a body cell is made of many organelles. There are some functions that are performed in conjunction with other organelles, but then there are certain tasks that an organelle can carry out on its own. In this way, the organelle serves as a subsystem to the cell as a whole.

Science is a highly-organized discipline. This organization stems on the fact that many parts of science share similar characteristics and are grouped accordingly. There are many sets of levels of organization that exists on Earth. These levels are based on large similarities and small differences. For example, all organisms are divided into one of the six kingdoms but are then further divided based on small differences from organisms in the main group. Concepts and investigations are also grouped in science. The results of an investigation can either be classified as evidence to a larger concept, a model of a system, or an explanation of a concept.

Parts of a system are grouped together because the parts work together on a common goal. Parts of science can also be grouped by its form or function. The definition of an organ is a group of tissues working together. For this reason, all organs can be grouped together because they all have the same basic make up. Of course they are very different and perform different functions, but their structure is the same.

There are many examples of systems and subsystems in the natural world. As previously mentioned a system can stand on its own and perform a function. Often there are smaller subsystems that make up a larger system. The subsystems perform a unique task on its own that is separate from the major system. Some of the subsystems interact with each other on common tasks as well.

History of Science

The development of science has been and will always be a collective effort. Individuals from all over the world with various backgrounds contribute to scientific developments. People have always wondered what makes up the world around us. Discoveries such as that of the atom and the cell have led to the discovery of many more elements on the periodic table and the structure of DNA.

Scientific theories and knowledge are constantly changing. As technology improves, current theories are tested under improved circumstances. An example of such an improvement surrounds the discovery of the atom.

> Dalton understood the basic concept of an atom, including atomic theory. However, scientists such as Thomson, Rutherford, and Bohr have made significant improvements to Dalton's original model. In fact, new discoveries have been made about atomic structure within the last ten years. Science is constantly evolving.

Science is a **subjective** area of study, largely based on the interests of those who are studying the concepts. It's largely a human endeavor influenced by societal, cultural, and personal views of the world. For example, a person's culture and background, as well as societal issues and biases, play key roles in determining scientific interests. Different countries have different focuses or areas they feel are important.

Ethics of Science

When conducting, analyzing, and publishing scientific investigations, there are certain ethics that must be followed. These ethical standards are accepted by the science community as a whole. The main standard is to always give credit when using someone else's work in your investigation.

The science community is very large and diverse, so it may be tempting to count someone's work as your own. However, this is never acceptable, and there are many ways of discovering and exposing plagiarism. Never risk your integrity – it's hard to ever come back from an incriminating event and regain creditability in the scientific community.

Applications of Science

One can apply scientific principles to analyze factors (e.g., diet, exercise, personal behavior) that influence personal and societal choices concerning fitness and health (e.g., physiological and psychological effects and risks associated with the use of substances and substance abuse). The scientific method can be used to solve almost any problem, concern, or wondering. These types of investigation rely heavily on observations.

Science makes logical conclusions, and therefore can help us make logical conclusions as well. One can apply scientific principles, the theory of probability, and risk/benefit analysis in order to analyze the advantages of, disadvantages of, or alternatives to a given decision or course of action.

Scientific principles such as Newton's Laws of Motion and the Bernoulli Principle are used constantly. The law of wearing safety belts, for example, is based upon Newton's First Law of Motion.

The Bernoulli Principle informs those who work in aeronautics the advantages and disadvantages of certain designs of aircrafts, and therefore ensures that aircrafts fly properly.

The scientific method can solve problems personal, societal, and global. You can increase your students' interest in science by giving examples of such problems. Take disease prevention, which is a huge concern. Researchers develop scientific experiments and field tests to determine the best method to controlling diseases. The West Nile Virus has proved to be a concern among many communities – but researchers have performed scientific investigations on how to control mosquitoes (and therefore the virus).

Natural Resources

Students may also be interested in understanding the role of science – and the role of humans – in affecting natural resources. There are two main groupings of natural resources: renewable and nonrenewable.

Renewable resources are those that can be replaced and managed. They are restored by nature and are therefore not in grave danger of depletion. Think of oxygen and water, for example. **Nonrenewable** resources, on the other hand, are lost once used. Examples include natural gas and other fossil fuels. Once these items are used up, there will be none left.

Human consumption of both renewable and nonrenewable resources is slowly becoming a problem. The renewable resources, although they replenish themselves, are being used faster than they can be replaced. As for nonrenewable resources, the dependency that has been developed on these materials is weighing heavy on society as a whole. Alternative methods and resources are being developed so that the consumption of nonrenewable products can decrease. Through scientific methods, solutions to these problems are being reached – showing once more how instrumental science is to the development and continuity of society.

Test Your Knowledge: Basic Principles of Science

1. You plan to perform a lab activity with your students that involves them mixing baking soda and vinegar. Make a list of possible safety precautions students should follow during this activity.

2. Convert 3.5 meters to kilometers.

3. When handling live specimens, it is important to use proper _________.

4. Which of the following numbers has the most significant figures?
   a) 3456
   b) 0.033
   c) 980
   d) 2010.0

5. Where is the best place to find information about the hazards of a chemical?
   a) The lab manual.
   b) MSDS.
   c) The textbook.
   d) The teacher manual.

6. If you are not certain how to properly use first aid, what should you do?

7. Which of the following is not considered safety equipment?
   a) Safety goggles.
   b) Eye wash.
   c) Test tube holder.
   d) Fire extinguisher.

8. Why is calibration important?

9. What is the most important thing to remember when performing a lab activity?

10. Look at the following data table a student constructed during science class. What is wrong with his data?

Time	Distance	Speed
1 min	2 meters	2 meters/min
2 min	4 meters	2 meters/min
3 min	7 meters	2.33 meters/min

11. Of the following answer choices, which ones can be answered by science?

a) Why is the sky blue?
b) Why does Sarah like blue better than pink?
c) Why are my eyes blue instead of brown?
d) Why does Jane like Michael?

12. True/False: There are no known variables in neither descriptive nor comparative investigations.

13. True/False: It is possible for a scientific report to be considered new knowledge if it has not been peer reviewed by members of the scientific community.

14. Briefly describe the characteristics of a system.

15. Choose a system in science that fits into the model of a system. Write out how the system fits into each of the five parts of the model.

16. What is the benefit of using a model?

17. Observe the following data. Which conclusion can be made based on this data?

Time	Distance	Speed
60 sec	2 meters	.03 meters/sec
120 sec	4 meters	.03 meters/sec
180 sec	7 meters	.039 meters/sec

a) As time increased, speed increased.
b) As distance increased, speed increased.
c) As distance and time increased, speed decreased.
d) As distance increased, speed remained about the same.

18. What are subsystems?

Test Your Knowledge: – Answers

1. There are many answers, which may include:
   - Always wear safety glasses (to protect the eyes from chemicals).
   - Always be careful when using glass containers (the chemicals could be stored in glass).
   - Do not lean over any open containers (foreign objects could end up in containers).
   - Waft over containers to smell the contents, never stick your nose in a container (some chemicals may be harmful if inhaled).

2. **0.0035 km**.

3. "**ethics**."

4. **d)** 2010.0 has five significant figures. Answer **a)** has four, and both **b)** and **c)** have two.

5. **b)**

6. You should take a **first aid class.**

7. **c)**

8. It ensures that your data output is **accurate and precise.**

9. **Safety**.

10. The **time** should be measured in **seconds**, **not minutes.**

11. Answers **a)** and **c)** can be answered by science, as there are scientific experiments that can be performed to answer them. Answers **b)** and **d)** are based on personal opinion and can therefore not be proven or answered by science.

12. **False**. Descriptive investigations do not have variables. Comparative investigations involve variables.

13. **False; once a scientific report is published, it has to be thoroughly reviewed by qualifying members of the science community before it can be considered new knowledge among the general public.**

14. Answers will vary, but should include information about **structure, action,** and **interconnectivity.**

15. **Answer will vary but there are many science systems that fit this criteria.**

16. Models allow you to study part of the natural world that cannot be studied in its natural state.

17. d)

18. Part of a larger system that can carry out functions independently.

Chapter 2: Molecular and Cellular Biology

We began learning the difference between living (**animate**) beings and nonliving (**inanimate**) objects from an early age. Living organisms and inanimate objects are all composed of **atoms** from elements. Those atoms are arranged into groups called **molecules**, which serve as the building blocks of everything in existence (as we know it). Molecular interactions are what determine whether something is classified as animate or inanimate.

Biomolecules

The human body, for example, needs many **chemical elements** that are necessary for life. The major elements are **Carbon, Hydrogen, Oxygen,** and **Nitrogen**. You can remember these elements by thinking of the acronym **CHON**. 96% of the human body is made of these elements.

Carbon: The majority of the chemical processes inside organisms are largely centered on carbon. For example, plants cannot perform photosynthesis (the process by which they make food) without carbon.

Hydrogen: Hydrogen is the smallest and most abundant of all elements. Because of its abundance, it is heavily used by living organisms. It also bonds rather easily with other elements, including carbon, making it another essential element for carrying out chemical processes within living organisms. For example, hydrogen bonds with chlorine to assist with digestion. Hydrogen and carbon are the elements most used by living organisms.

Oxygen: Found not only in the air but also in water, oxygen is important to living beings because it fuels the cells of the body which supply the body with energy. For this reason, most organisms rely on oxygen to live.

Nitrogen: Nitrogen is the prime ingredient in amino acids, which create proteins, which contain the cells responsible for holding genetic information about an organism. Plants obtain nitrogen from the soil, and animals must meet their nitrogen needs by eating plants or eating other plant-eating animals.

There are other minor, yet necessary, elements in the human body including Calcium, Phosphorus, Potassium, Sulfur, Sodium, Chlorine, and Magnesium. The chart below shows what percent of the body is made of the minor elements.

Element(s)	Percentage in the Body (by mass)
Ca	1.5%
P	1%
K	0.35%
S	0.25%
Na	0.15%
Mg	0.05%
Cu, Zn, Se, Mo, F, Cl, I, Ma, Co, Fe	0.7%
Li, Sr, Al, Si, Pb, V, As, Br	Trace amounts

Another way to describe living and nonliving things is through the terms **organic** and **inorganic.**

- **Organic molecules** are from living organisms. Organic molecules contain **carbon-hydrogen bonds**.

- **Inorganic molecules** come from non-living resources. They do not contain carbon-hydrogen bonds. This does not, however, make them unnecessary for organic beings to consume. Water, for example, is inorganic – it is also absolutely essential for human life.

The **synthesis** (or creation) of new biomolecules such as proteins, lipids, carbohydrates, and nucleic acids can only occur through one or more **chemical reactions**. Chemical reactions are a series of changes that take place in order to create something new. The same holds true when a biomolecule is being degraded. When a biomolecule is going through **degradation**, it is being broken down through a series of chemical reactions.

There are four major classes of organic biomolecules: Carbohydrates, Lipids, Proteins, and Nucleic Acids. The chart below reviews their structure and function.

Biomolecule	Major Elements	Function
Carbohydrates	C, H, O	Breaks down fatty acids, regulates energy by serving as a temporary energy storage, provide sugar
Lipids	C, H, O	Serve as an energy storage, provide cells and organelles with a membrane, provide the body with hormones and vitamins
Proteins	C, H, N, O	Involved in all cellular functions, specific functions vary based on the type of protein
Nucleic Acids	C, H, N, O, P	Pass on hereditary information to genes and pass information to other cell structures so that they may carry out biological processes

Carbohydrates consist of only hydrogen, oxygen, and carbon atoms. They are the most abundant single class of organic substances found in nature. Carbohydrate molecules provide many basic necessities such as: fiber, vitamins, and minerals; structural components for organisms, especially plants; and, perhaps most importantly, energy. Our bodies break down carbohydrates to make **glucose**: a sugar used to produce that energy which our bodies need in order to operate. Brain cells are exclusively dependent upon a constant source of glucose molecules.

There are two kinds of carbohydrates: simple and complex. **Simple carbohydrates** can be absorbed directly through the cell, and therefore enter the blood stream very quickly. We consume simple carbohydrates in dairy products, fruits, and other sugary foods.

Complex carbohydrates consist of a chain of simple sugars which, over time, our bodies break down into simple sugars (which are also referred to as stored energy.) **Glycogen** is the storage form of glucose in human and animal cells. Complex carbohydrates come from starches like cereal, bread, beans, potatoes, and starchy vegetables.

Lipids, commonly known as fats, are molecules with two functions:

1. They are stored as an energy reserve.

2. They provide a protective cushion for vital organs.

In addition to those two functions, lipids also combine with other molecules to form essential compounds, such as **phospholipids,** which form the membranes around cells. Lipids also combine with other molecules to create naturally-occurring **steroid** hormones, like the hormones estrogen and testosterone.

Proteins are large molecules which our bodies' cells need in order to function properly. Consisting of **amino acids,** proteins aid in maintaining and creating many aspects of our cells: cellular structure, function, and regulation, to name a few. Proteins also work as neurotransmitters and carriers of oxygen in the blood (hemoglobin).

Without protein, our tissues and organs could not exist. Our muscles bones, skin, and many other parts of the body contain significant amounts of protein. **Enzymes**, hormones, and antibodies are proteins.

Enzymes

When heat is applied, chemical reactions are typically sped up. However, the amount of heat required to speed up reactions could be potentially harmful (even fatal) to living organisms. Instead, our bodies use molecules called enzymes to bring reactants closer together, causing them to form a new compound. Thus, the whole reaction rate is increased without heat. Even better – the enzymes are not consumed during the reaction process, and can therefore be used reused. This makes them an important biochemical part of both photosynthesis and respiration.

Nucleic acids are large molecules made up of smaller molecules called **nucleotides.** **DNA** (deoxyribonucleic acid) transports and transmits genetic information. As you can tell from the name, DNA is a nucleic acid. Since nucleotides make up nucleic acids, they are considered the basis of reproduction and progression.

The normal functioning of living organisms, and the activities by which life is maintained, are both studied in physiology. This study includes such things as cell activity, tissues, and organs; as well as processes such as muscle movement, nervous systems, nutrition, digestion, respiration, circulation, and reproduction.

One characteristic of living things is the performance of chemical reactions collectively called metabolism. Cells, the basic units of life, perform many metabolic reactions. In multi-celled organisms, cells group together and form tissues that enable the organisms' functions. Tissues group together and form organs, which in turn work together in an organ system.

Cells, Tissues, and Organs

All organisms are composed of microscopic cells, although the type and number of cells may vary. A cell is the minimum amount of organized living matter that is complex enough to carry out the functions of life. This section will briefly review both animal and plant cells, noting their basic similarities and differences.

Cell Structure

Around the cell is the **cell membrane**, which separates the living cell from the rest of the environment and regulates the comings and goings of molecules within the cell. Because the cell membrane allows some molecules to pass through while blocking others, it is considered **semipermeable.** Each cell's membrane communicates and interacts with the membranes of other cells. In additional to a cell membrane, *plants* also have a **cell wall** which is necessary for structural support and protection. Animal cells do not contain a cell wall.

Organelle

Cells are filled with a gelatin-like substance called **protoplasm** which contains various structures called **organelles**; called so because they act like small versions of organs. The diagram on the next page illustrates the basic organelles of both a plant and an animal cell. Pay attention to the differences and similarities between the two.

PLANT CELL (A)

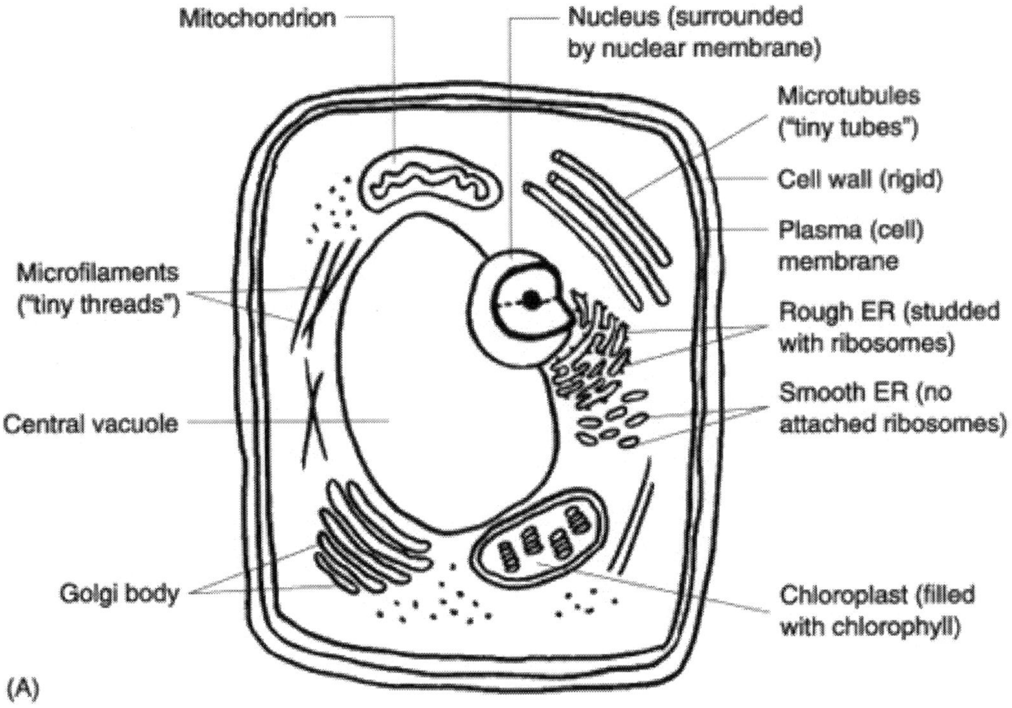

ANIMAL CELL (B)[1]

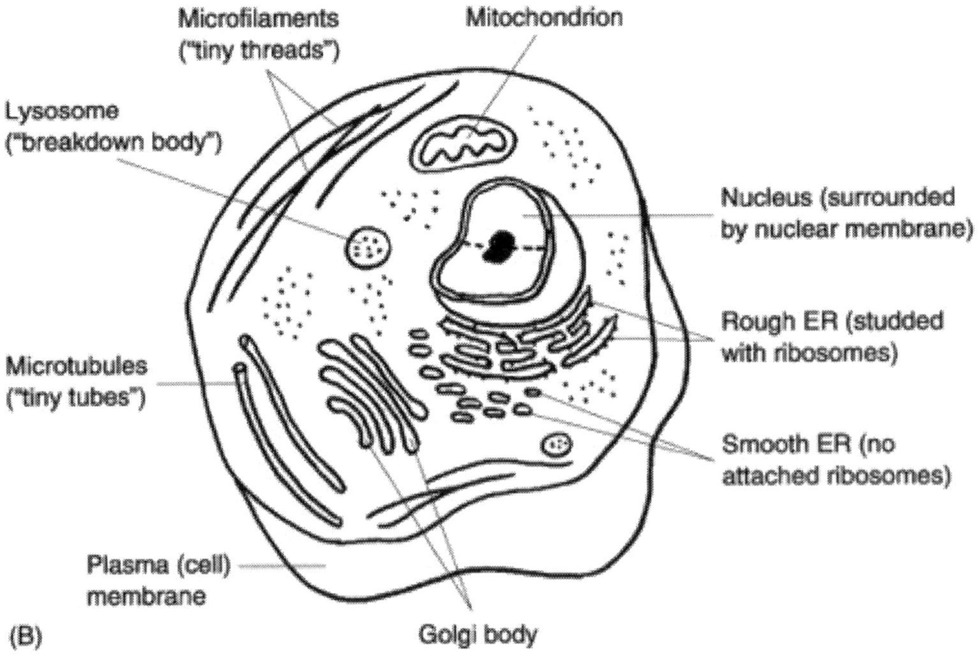

[1] Graphics from: http://www.education.com

Mitochondria are spherical or rod-shaped organelles which carry out the reactions of aerobic respiration. They are the power generators of both plant and animal cells, because they convert oxygen and nutrients into ATP, the chemical energy that powers the cell's metabolic activities.

Ribosomes are extremely tiny spheres that make proteins. These proteins are used either as enzymes or as support for other cell functions.

The **Golgi Apparatus** is essential to the production of polysaccharides (carbohydrates), and made up of a layered stack of flattened sacs.

The **Endoplasmic Reticulum** is important in the synthesis and packaging of proteins. It is a complex system of internal membranes, and is called either rough (when ribosomes are attached), or smooth (no ribosomes attached).

Chloroplasts are only found in plants. They contain the chlorophyll molecule necessary for photosynthesis.

The **Nucleus** controls all of the cell's functions, and contains the all-important genetic information, or DNA, of a cell.

Cellular Differentiation

Single-celled organisms have only one cell to carry out all of their required biochemical and structural functions. On the other hand, multi-celled organisms – except for very primitive ones (i.e. sponges) – have various groups of cells called **tissues** that each perform specific functions (**differentiation**).

There are four main types of tissues: **epithelial**, **connective, muscular,** and **nervous**.

Epithelial tissue is made up groups of flattened cells which are grouped tightly together to form a solid surface. Those cells are arranged in one or many layer(s) to form an external or internal covering of the body or organs. Epithelial tissue protects the body from injury and allows for the exchange of gases in the lungs and bronchial tubes. There's even a form of epithelial tissue that produces eggs and sperm, an organism's sex cells.

Connective tissue is made of cells which are surrounded by non-cellular material. For example, bones contain some cells, but they are also surrounded by a considerable amount of non-cellular, extracellular material.

Muscular tissue has the ability to contract. There are three types:

1. **Cardiac** tissue, found in the heart.

2. **Smooth** tissue, located in the walls of hollow internal structures such as blood vessels, the stomach, intestines, and urinary bladder.

3. **Skeletal** (or striated) tissue, found in the muscles.

Nervous tissue consists of cells called **neurons.** Neurons specialize in making many connections with and transmitting electrical impulses to each other. The brain, spinal cord, and peripheral nerves are all made of nervous tissue.

Organs and Organ Systems

As living organisms go through their life cycle, they grow and/or develop. Single-celled organisms grow and develop very rapidly; whereas complex, multi-celled organisms take much longer to progress. All organisms go through changes as they age. These changes involve the development of more complex functions, which in turn require groups of tissues to form larger units called **organs.**

Examples of Organs

1. **The heart** - made of cardiac muscle and conjunctive tissue (conjunctive tissue makes up the valves), the heart pumps blood first to the lungs in order to pick up oxygen, then through the rest of the body to deliver the oxygen, and finally back to the lungs to start again.

2. **Roots** - A tree's are covered by an epidermis which is in turn made up of a protective tissue. They are also *composed* of tissue, which allows them to grow. The root organ also contains **conductive tissue** to absorb and transport water and nutrients to the rest of the plant.

Generally, in complex organisms like plants and animals, many organs are grouped together into **systems.** For example, many combinations of tissues make up the many organs which create the digestive system in animals. The organs in the digestive system consist of the mouth, the esophagus, the stomach, small and large intestines, the liver, the pancreas, and the gall bladder.

Structure and Function

As you will see in multiple disciplines, structure and function are always tightly related. Function depends upon proper structure, just as structure exists for the purpose of a function. In biology, this is particularly relevant in cells – in fact, there are differences in cell structure and function, not just among the cells in a single body, but between different types of organisms. For instance, look at the cells found in humans and plants – which we refer to as **eukaryotic** – and those in bacteria (**prokaryotic**).

Cell Type

Both prokaryotic and eukaryotic cells are made up of smaller components (referred to as organelles in eukaryotic cells). Study the chart below. Note the differences in structure between the different cell types, and think about what that signifies for the function.

Cell Type	Structure	Function	Example
Viruses	Contains DNA and protective wall.	Nonliving cell that binds to a host and replicates.	Common cold.
Prokaryotic Cells	Does not contain membrane-bound organelles.	In many cases, these cells serve as the entire "body" of an organism.	Bacteria.
Eukaryotic Cells	Contains a true nucleus and membrane-bound organelles.	Contains organelles that perform many functions that are essential for the cells' survival.	Cells within multicellular organisms such as plants and humans.

Earlier in our review, we covered organelles – the components of plant and animal cells – and looked at a diagram detailing the differences between plant and animal cells. Analyze the following chart to see the different components between prokaryotic and eukaryotic cells.

Components of Prokaryotic and Eukaryotic Cells

Cell Component	Prokaryotic (P), Eukaryotic (E), or Both (B)	Main Function
Cell membrane	B	Selects what enters or leaves the cell.
Cell wall	B	Protects plant cells and provides structure to plants.
Ribosomes	B	Produce proteins to be used either inside or outside of the cell.
Nucleus	E	Controls the cells. Gives instructions to the other parts of the cell.

Mitochondrion	E	Provide the cell with energy.
Cytoplasm	B	Jelly-like fluid that contains necessary molecules needed for specialized functions, provide the cell with shape.
Chloroplast	E	Help produce food in plant cells.

Cell Structure

It's important for you to be able to identify differences in cell structure and function in different types of organisms; right now, let's look again at the differences between plant and animal cells.

Both plant and animal cells are eukaryotic, and they both have very similar organelles. However, those organelles – though technically the same – often have different appearances and structures. Even still, some organelles are unique to both plant and animal cells.

Cell Structure of Plant and Animal Cells

Cell Structure	Animal Cells	Plant Cells
Cell Membrane	Present	Present
Cell Wall	Absent	Present
Centrioles	Present	Only Present in a Few
Chloroplast	Absent	Present
Cilia	Present	Rarely Present
Cytoplasm	Present	Present
Endoplasmic Reticulum	Present	Present
Flagella	Found in Some	Found in Some
Golgi Apparatus	Present	Present
Lysosome	Present	Rarely Present
Microtubules	Present	Present
Mitochondria	Present	Present
Nucleus	Present	Present
Plastids	Absent	Present
Ribosomes	Present	Present
Vacuole	One or More Small Vacuoles	One Large Vacuole

Remember the following:

- The **cell wall** provides plant cells with structure and support.
- **Centrioles** are used to help organize microtubules during cell division of animal plants.
- **Cilia** assist with the movement of cells.
- **Chloroplasts** are unique to plant cells because they assist the plant with making its own food. Animals do not make their own food.
- **Lysosomes** are responsible for breaking down particles within the animal cell. Lysosomes can also break down the cell itself if needed.
- **Plastids** make and store food inside plant cells.

The eukaryotic cells in both plants and animals are highly **specialized**. This means that they are formulated to perform certain tasks. Let's look at the specialization of structure and function in different types of cells in animals and plants.

Animals

There are many different types of specialized animal cells. Here are a few of the major types:

- **Skin Cells**: Make up a larger structure of tissue called epithelial tissue. This tissue covers the majority of the body, serving as the first layer of defense for the body.

- **Nerve Cells**: Make up the brain and other parts of the nervous system. They are responsible for transmitting information to all parts of the body.

- **Muscle Cells**: Make up muscle tissue and are responsible for muscle contraction and movement.

Plants

Just like animals, plants have many specialized cells. A few of the most commonly-known are:

- **Root Cells**: Responsible for the management of gases into and out of the plant, as well as the flow of water.

- **Stem Cells**: Most noted for their tasks of supplying the plant with the cells responsible for tissues and organs.

- **Leaf Cells**: Cover the leaves of plants and are responsible for carrying out the process of photosynthesis.

Life Processes

Single-celled organisms excrete toxic substances either by diffusion through their cell membranes, or through specialized organelles called **vacuoles.** When metabolic chemical reactions occur within the cells of organisms, wastes are produced that could cause harm to the body. Those wastes therefore must be excreted. Multicellular organisms require special organ systems – humans specifically utilize the circulatory and excretory systems – to eliminate wastes.

Organisms need to be able to respond to changes in their external environment, all the while still maintaining a relatively constant internal environment. They must maintain a balance of water, temperature, and salt concentration, to name just a few. The physical and chemical processes that work to maintain an internal balance are called **homeostasis**. In humans, homeostasis is maintained by the cooperation of both the circulatory and the renal systems.

During digestion, food is broken down, absorbed as very small molecules, and carried to the cells by blood.

Cells need these broken-down molecules to perform the life-sustaining biochemical reactions of metabolism, which produce wastes.

1. **Aerobic respiration** produces water and **carbon dioxide**.
2. **Anaerobic respiration** produces **lactic acid** and carbon dioxide.
3. Dehydration synthesis produces water.
4. Protein metabolism produces **nitrogenous wastes**, (i.e. **ammonia**).
5. Other metabolic processes can produce salts, oils, etc.

When a cell is in **homeostasis**, it is said to be in equilibrium or good working order. Remember, the cell membrane is extremely selective of what enters the cell and what leaves the cell. It allows material to come in when needed and, if the cell is too full, allows unnecessary items to exit. Homeostasis is also maintained by the processes of diffusion, osmosis, and filtration.

- **Diffusion** requires no energy and moves items down its **concentration gradient**, where items of a high concentration are moved to an area of low concentration.

- **Osmosis** is the diffusion of water. Water moves from an area of high concentration to an area of low concentration

- **Filtration** occurs when the pores within the cell membrane reject small materials that are not needed by the cell.

- The **rate of movement** for all methods is dependent upon the **surface area** of which the material must be moved. As the concentration difference rises, the rate of movement increases.

Diffusion and osmosis serve as the primary way that cells transport water, nutrients and wastes across cell membranes. Some cells also have **transport systems** made up of proteins that are selectively permeable to a wide variety of material.

Cellular Respiration
As you can imagine, there are a great deal of processes which require energy: breathing, blood circulation, body temperature control, muscle usage, digestion, brain and nerve functioning are all only a few examples. You can refer to all of the body's physical and chemical processes which convert or use energy as **metabolism**.

All living things in the world, including plants, require energy in order to maintain their metabolisms. Initially, that energy is consumed through food. That energy is processed in plants and animals through **photosynthesis** (for plants) and **respiration** (for animals). **Cellular respiration** produces the actual energy molecules known as **ATP** (Adenosine Tri-Phosphate) molecules.

Plants use ATP during **photosynthesis** for producing glucose, which is then broken down during cellular respiration. This cycle continuously repeats itself throughout the life of the plant.

Photosynthesis: Plants, as well as some Protists and Monerans, can use light energy to bind together small molecules from the environment. These newly-bound molecules are then used as fuel to make more energy. This process is called photosynthesis, and one of its byproducts is none other than oxygen. Most organisms, including plants, require oxygen to fuel the biochemical reactions of metabolism.

You can see in the following equation that plants use the energy taken from light to turn carbon dioxide and water – the small molecules from their environment – into glucose and oxygen.

The photosynthesis equation:

$$\underset{\text{Carbon Dioxide}}{\mathbf{CO2}} + \underset{\text{Water}}{\mathbf{H2O}} \xrightarrow{\textbf{Light}} \underset{\text{Glucose (sugar)}}{\mathbf{C6H12O6}} + \underset{\text{Oxygen}}{\mathbf{O2}}$$

Chlorophyll
In order for photosynthesis to occur, however, plants require a specific molecule to capture sunlight. This molecule is called **chlorophyll**. When chlorophyll absorbs sunlight, one of its electrons is stimulated into a higher energy state. This higher-energy electron then passes that energy onto other electrons in other molecules, creating a chain that eventually results in glucose. Chlorophyll absorbs red and blue light, but not green; green light is reflected off of plants, which is why plants appear green to us. It's important to note that chlorophyll is absolutely necessary to the photosynthesis process in plants –if it photosynthesizes, it will have chlorophyll.

The really fascinating aspect of photosynthesis is that raw sunlight energy is a very nonliving thing; however, it is still absorbed by plants to form the chemical bonds between simple inanimate compounds. This produces organic sugar, which is the chemical basis for the formation of all living compounds. Isn't it amazing? Something nonliving is essential to the creation of all living things!

Respiration

Respiration is the metabolic opposite of photosynthesis. There are two types of respiration: **aerobic** (which uses oxygen) and **anaerobic** (which occurs without the use of oxygen).

You may be confused at thinking of the word "respiration" in this way, since many people use respiration to refer to the process of breathing. However, in biology, breathing is thought of as **inspiration** (inhaling) and **expiration** (exhalation); whereas **respiration** is the metabolic, chemical reaction supporting these processes. Both plants and animals produce carbon dioxide through respiration.

Aerobic respiration is the reaction which uses enzymes to combine oxygen with organic matter (food). This yields carbon dioxide, water, and energy.

The respiration equation looks like this:

$$C6H12O6 + 6O2 \xrightarrow{\textbf{Enzymes}} 7\ 6CO2 + 6H2O + \text{energy}$$

If you look back the equation for photosynthesis, you will see that respiration is almost the same equation, only it goes in the opposite direction. (Photosynthesis uses carbon dioxide and water, with the help of energy, to create oxygen and glucose. Respiration uses oxygen and glucose, with the help of enzymes, to create carbon dioxide, water, and energy.)

Anaerobic respiration is respiration that occurs WITHOUT the use of oxygen. It produces less energy than aerobic respiration produces, yielding only two molecules of ATP per glucose molecule Aerobic respiration produces 38 ATP per glucose molecule.

So, plants convert energy into matter and release oxygen gas – animals then absorb this oxygen gas in order to run their own metabolic reaction and, in the process, release carbon dioxide. That carbon dioxide is then absorbed by plants in the photosynthetic conversion of energy into matter. Everything comes full circle! This is called a **metabolic cycle.**

Growth and Development

Cells are constantly growing and replicating through processes called cell cycles. **Growth factors** are proteins that regulate cell division. These proteins will attach to the cell membrane, triggering cell division to begin. Cells do not replicate until they have reached a mature size. During the maturation phase, the cell cycle is in a **growth**, or **G, phase**.

Defects can occur to cause cell growth to become unregulated. Sometimes DNA in the body can be damaged. Under normal circumstances, DNA replication stops while a gene triggers enzymes to repair the damaged portion of the DNA. Those repaired continue to replicate, while those that remain damaged are demolished.

If the gene responsible for triggering the enzymes to fix damaged DNA is abnormal, the damaged DNA continues to replicate. These damaged cells could then accumulate more damage along the way and become unstoppable. The result is **cancer** - unregulated cell growth.

The following factors have the potential to affect cell differentiation, as well as the growth and development of organisms:

Genetics
There are some genetic disorders which can be inherited, or can be the result of a mutation. These disorders affect how certain cells grow and develop.

Disease
Diseases and viruses develop when foreign cells come into the body, attach themselves to a host cell, and replicate. Once this replication occurs, the diseased cells take over the function of the normal cells.

Nutrition
Cells need proper nutrients in order to differentiate and grow properly. Improper nutrition can cause multiple cell types to function improperly.

Toxic Chemicals
An organism's DNA can be damaged when that organism is exposed to toxic chemicals or radiation. DNA is involved in cell growth, and complications could develop if damaged DNA continues to replicate.

Organization in the Body

The human body has five different **levels of organization**. In fact, most multicellular organisms contain these levels of organization. The five levels are:

Cells

The first and most basic level is the cell. Not all cells are created equal. They vary based on structure and function. Those cells that perform the same function come together and work on a common task.

Tissue

When cells come together for the same function, they form a tissue. Tissues together then form an organ. Organs together form organ systems. An organism is a collection of multiple organ systems. There are four main types of tissue in the human body: epithelial tissue, muscle tissue, nervous tissue, and connective tissue.

Organs
When a group of tissue works together on a common task, they form an organ. Some organs function in more than one organ system.

Organ Systems
When a group of organs work together on a common task, they form an organ system. The human body itself houses twelve major organ systems: Circulatory, Digestive, Endocrine, Integumentary, Lymphatic, Immune, Muscular, Nervous, Reproductive, Respiratory, Skeletal, and Urinary.

Organisms
When a group of organ systems work together in order to maintain homeostasis, they form an organism.

Test Your Knowledge: Molecular and Cellular Biology

1. Life depends upon:
    a) The bond energy in molecules.
    b) The energy of protons.
    c) The energy of electrons.
    d) The energy of neutrons.

2. Which of the following elements is **NOT** found in carbohydrates?
    a) Carbon.
    b) Hydrogen.
    c) Oxygen.
    d) Sulfur.

3. Which of the following is a carbohydrate molecule?
    a) Amino acid.
    b) Glycogen.
    c) Sugar.
    d) Lipid.

4. Lipids are commonly known as:
    a) Fat.
    b) Sugar.
    c) Enzymes.
    d) Protein.

5. Proteins are composed of:
    a) Nucleic acids.
    b) Amino acids.
    c) Hormones.
    d) Lipids.

6. Which statement is true about Earth's organisms?
    a) All organisms are based on the cell as the basic unit of life.
    b) Protists are an exception to the cell theory and are not based on cells.
    c) Only single-celled organisms are based on cells.
    d) All organisms are based on tissues as the basic unit of life.

7. What organelle produces the cell's energy source?
    a) Chloroplast.
    b) Nucleus.
    c) Mitochondrion.
    d) Endoplasmic reticulum.

8. The formation of tissue depends upon:
    a) Cell differentiation.
    b) Cell membranes.
    c) Cell death.
    d) Cell organelles.

9. Cardiac muscle is an example of what tissue?

a) Smooth muscle.
b) Nervous.
c) Contractile.
d) Connective.

10. Which organelle has two forms: rough and smooth?

a) Mitochondrion.
b) Golgi apparatus.
c) Nucleus.
d) Endoplasmic reticulum.

11. Which organelle is important in the production of polysaccharides (carbohydrates)?

a) Mitochondrion.
b) Golgi apparatus.
c) Nucleus.
d) Endoplasmic reticulum.

12. Which of the following is **NOT** true of enzymes?

a) Enzymes are lipid molecules.
b) Enzymes are not consumed in a biochemical reaction.
c) Enzymes are important in photosynthesis and respiration.
d) Enzymes speed up reactions and make them more efficient.

13. Plants appear green because chlorophyll:

a) Absorbs green light.
b) Reflects red light.
c) Absorbs blue light.
d) Reflects green light.

14. Photosynthesis is the opposite of:

a) Enzymatic hydrolysis.
b) Protein synthesis.
c) Respiration.
d) Reproduction.

15. The compound that absorbs light energy during photosynthesis is:

a) Chloroform.
b) Chlorofluorocarbon.
c) Chlorinated biphenyls.
d) Chlorophyll.

16. What is the name of the sugar molecule produced during photosynthesis?

a) Chlorophyll
b) Glycogen
c) Glucose
d) Fructose

Test Your Knowledge: Cell Structure and Processes – Answers

1. **a)**
2. **d)**
3. **c)**
4. **a)**
5. **b)**
6. **a)**
7. **c)**
8. **a)**
9. **c)**
10. **d)**
11. **b)**
12. **a)**
13. **d)**
14. **c)**
15. **d)**
16. **c)**

Chapter 3: Classical Genetics and Evolution & Ecology

Heredity is the study of how traits are passed from parent to offspring, and is essentially the basis for diversity of life. In order to teach about life and its diversity, you must first understand the basic foundation on which it is built.

Nucleic Acids

Nucleic acids are polymers that consist of **nucleotides**. There are two types of nucleic acids. **Deoxyribonucleic acid (DNA)** and **ribonucleic acid (RNA)** are named based on the type of five-carbon sugar they contain. DNA is a double-helix polymer consisting of the nitrogenous bases cytosine (C), adenine (A), guanine (G), and thymine (T). The two strands of the helix are complementary, so one strand can always be a template for the other. This property allows DNA to replicate itself, providing a mechanism for propagating life.

Guanine pairs with Cytosine

Adenine pairs with Thymine

Genes are segments of DNA that pass down from parent to offspring; they transfer traits. Units of genes are organized as **chromosomes**. Humans have 23 pairs of chromosomes. One pair comes from the father, and another from the mother. Chromosomes are found in the nucleus of cells. While this is a great amount of information to fit within the cell's small nucleus, a combination of DNA with protein called **chromatin** compacts the DNA into a small package, allowing DNA to fit inside the nucleus of the cell.

STUDY TIP: In eukaryotic cells, the DNA is found in the nucleus, coiled into chromosomes. Because prokaryotes lack a nucleus, the DNA either attaches to the cell membrane or floats freely in the cell. Chromatin is only found in eukaryotic cells.

The two strands of DNA are held together via hydrogen bonds; when DNA replicates, the enzyme **helicase** breaks those bonds, causing them to separate (the area of separation is called the **replication fork**). To replicate, the bases pair according to the complementary rule, and another enzyme bonds the DNA back together.

RNA has three types: mRNA (messenger), rRNA (ribosomal), and tRNA (transfer). Instead of thymine (T), RNA contains uracil (U).

STUDY TIP: RNA carries the genetic information out of the nucleus and into the cytoplasm.

Gene expression can be broken down into transcription and translation. **Transcription** is the process of converting the genetic code from DNA to mRNA. **Translation** is the conversion of the code from RNA into proteins.

Despite the replication process, changes to genes can still occur. **Mutations** are such changes made to the genes or the genetic code. This can occur for many reasons: environmental factors, such as exposure to radiation; exposure to chemical compounds, ultraviolet light, and free radicals; and more. Mutated genes are passed on to every cell that develops from it. However, not all mutations are bad. While some can have harmful effects, others can have little-to-no impact, and still others could be beneficial to the organism. When an organism reproduces sexually, only mutations within the sperm or egg are passed on to the offspring.

Some of the changes that may occur in a mutation include base-pair substitution, base insertion, and base deletion.

> In a **base-pair substitution**, one nucleotide base is replaced with another. This could lead to one amino acid being substituted for another during protein synthesis. Sickle cell anemia is an example of a genetic disorder caused by base-pair substitution.
>
> In **base insertion**, an extra nucleotide base is added into the DNA sequence.
>
> In **base deletion**, one nucleotide base is removed from the DNA sequence. The addition or deletion of a base results in an abnormal protein to be synthesized.

There are several methods and applications for genetic identification and manipulations, and several advances have been made in medicine and forensics using DNA. For example, some genetic diseases can be cured simply by replacing a damaged gene with an inserted "fixed" gene. As DNA is remarkably individual, DNA can be used in forensics – through blood or hair samples – or in fingerprinting to identify people. In agriculture, DNA technology can be used to produce plants that have more desirable characteristics, such as a higher disease-resistance or nutritional value.

We have also utilized **recombinant DNA** technology to analyze genetic changes. In this process, DNA molecules are cut, spliced, and inserted into different bacteria to rapidly grow and divide. Think about the positive effects of this kind of process! For instance, human insulin – often in high-demand and absolutely crucial for a healthy life – is mass-produced through this process.

All normal cells reproduce via **mitosis**, which produces two cells that are identical to the parent cell. These two cells are called **diploids** and each contains a complete set of chromosomes (both always have the same number of chromosomes).

Sex cells (**gametes**) are produced in a different process, called **meiosis**, wherein the gametes are produced in such a manner that reduces the number of chromosomes in the cell by half. Think about it: If gametes had all of the sets of chromosomes, then after fertilization the zygote would have twice as many chromosomes as it is supposed to! Therefore, we need meiosis to ensure that each sex cell only has one of each pair of the chromosomes. This is referred to as a **haploid** number of chromosomes.

Continuity and Variation of Traits

To summarize what we've just covered above, the nucleic acids DNA and RNA transmit hereditary information. Each species has an original code within the double-strand of bases (called a **helix**) held together by hydrogen bonds.

Heredity is the term for the transmission of traits from parent to offspring. However, the results of this transmission are not completely random; in fact, we can attempt to predict genetic crosses through the use of **probability**. First discovered by Gregor Mendel for its use in genetics, **probability** is the likelihood of something to occur. In this case, we'll talk about the probability of certain traits.

Traits are the individual characteristics of an organism. Traits can be referred to as **dominant** or **recessive**. **Alleles**, generally found in pairs, are the different forms of genes. Dominant alleles contain traits more likely to be expressed and are written with capital letters. Recessive alleles contain those traits that are least likely to be expressed, and are written with lowercase letters.

There are multiple combinations possible with alleles. The two most important to remember are **homozygous** and **heterozygous**.

The root ***homos*** means "same." Think "homonym," which means "same-name," or "homophonic," meaning "same sound." Knowing this, you can remember that ***homozygous*** means "same-alleles." For example, if an offspring inherits two dominant alleles from its parents (written as AA), the alleles are homozygous dominant. If the offspring inherits two recessive alleles (aa), it is homozygous recessive.

On the other hand, ***heterozygous*** contains the root ***hetero***, meaning "different." Having one dominant and one recessive allele (Aa) is heterozygous.

When two parents with a single trait are crossed it is called a **monohybrid cross**.

There are two terms which are essential to the understanding of genetic probability: phenotype and genotype.

Phenotype is the physical characteristic of an organism. Think "**ph**eno → **ph**ysical" to remember this distinction. The phenotype is determined by how many have at least one dominant allele and how many have two recessive alleles.

On the other hand, **genotype** is the term used to describe the genetic makeup of the organism. "**Gen**o → **gen**etic." The genotype is determined by how many of the offspring would be homozygous dominant, then heterozygous, then homozygous recessive.

Genotypes and phenotypes can both be expressed as ratios.

Punnett squares are used to show which alleles are dominant and which are recessive; and, importantly, to predict the potential outcome for the offspring. While each parent would have two alleles for each trait, only one of those alleles will be donated during gamete formation. (That way, the child will also have two alleles: one from each parent.) This is known as the **law of segregation**.

See the following Punnett square for an example. One parent is homozygous recessive for blue eyes (bb), while the other is heterozygous for brown eyes (Bb). The possible results are shaded.

	Blue Eyes (b)	Blue Eyes (b)
Brown Eyes (B)	Bb	Bb
Blue Eyes (b)	Bb	bb

From the square, we can see that the parents have a 50% chance of producing offspring with brown eyes, and a 50% chance of producing offspring with blue eyes.

Co-dominance occurs when both genes are equally expressed. In this case, there are technically no recessive alleles – and all letters are capital in order to specify the allele.

Incomplete dominance is the blending – or intermediate form – of the traits. For example, red flowers and white flowers join together to produce pink flowers.

Oftentimes, genes can have more than two alleles controlling a trait, something which results in **multiple alleles**.

> Look at human blood types. There are four types of blood, indicated by the letters, A, B, AB, and O. A person would have the A blood type if they possess AA or AO. A person would have B blood type if they possess the alleles BB or BO. A person with AB blood type would have the AB alleles. For O blood type, a person would have to have OO alleles.

Blood Type:	A	B	AB	O
Necessary Alleles:	AA or AO	BB or BO	AB	OO

For humans, the 23rd pair of chromosomes determines sex. For males, the 23rd pair is XY; and for females, it is XX. The Y chromosome is missing some of the alleles, and is smaller than the X chromosome. This indicates that males only have to have one allele to get some recessive traits. Females would need to receive two alleles.

Some traits are transmitted on the sex chromosomes. This is referred to as **sex-linked inheritance**. Hemophilia and color blindness are two examples of such.

Theory for Biological Evolution

An **adaption** is a characteristic that gives an organism a better chance at survival or reproduction. Adaptions develop through **natural selection**, a word which also refers to the process through which populations become better suited to their environment. (This happens through a change in a trait that affects survival or reproduction within the population.) Over time, **natural selection** results in changes to populations and species. Many small changes over long periods of time eventually results in the evolution of large changes, a concept known as **gradualism**.

For example, the jaw bones in snakes have adapted in such a way that they can drop away from the skull – this allows them to eat larger prey. How did this trait get passed on? Through natural selection: Those snakes with this ability (at first in a smaller capacity, perhaps as a form of a mutation) were able to eat more, and therefore survived and reproduced more than the "normal" snakes.

One of the characteristics of reproductive success in a population is the **fitness** of an individual. (See above. The snake was more **fit** to survive.) The average number of offspring is also a factor of fitness.

The offspring of a fit individual can ensure natural selection within a population. **Variation** in the number of offspring produced in a population as the result of competition for mates is called **sexual selection**. Sexual selection is a type of natural selection.

Mutation and sexual recombination produce variations that make evolution possible. Only the mutations that are transmitted to the gamete can be passed on to the offspring, which can immediately change the gene pool by introducing a new allele. Sexual recombination, also called genetic recombination, is the process of forming new variations of alleles to produce a unique set of genetic material. Sexual recombination also produces genetic variation.

Natural selection, as well as **genetic drift** and **gene flow**, can alter a population's genetic composition.

> Natural selection is based on differential reproductive success.
>
> Genetic drift results from chance fluctuations in allele frequencies within small populations.
>
> Gene flow, or genetic exchange due to migration, may result in a population gaining or losing alleles. It tends to reduce differences between populations.

The three modes of natural selection are **directional, disruptive, and stabilizing selection**.

> **Directional selection** is most common during periods of environmental change, or when individuals in a population migrate into an area with different environmental conditions. This shifts the frequency curve for a phenotype character in one direction, because it favors the individuals who deviate from the average.

Disruptive selection happens when the environmental conditions favor members of a population at the extremes of a phenotype range, instead of those in the intermediate phenotypes. This can be important in the early stages of speciation. (We'll cover speciation more thoroughly in just a sec!)

Stabilizing selection, on the other hand, favors the intermediate phenotypes and acts against the extreme phenotypes. This reduces variation and maintains the status quo for a particular trait.

Speciation is the event that results in two or more species. There are a few processes that can lead to speciation. **Geographic isolation** is one process that can result in speciation. In those (and other) cases, populations are isolated from each other. There would therefore by a minimal exchange of genetic material between these two populations. Instead, breeding would occur within the separate populations themselves. This kind of circumstance could result in two different types of species, which originally came from a common ancestor.

Reduction of gene flow can also result in speciation. This occurs in populations where mating is not random. **Founder effect** is the loss of genetic variation when a population has a small number of individuals. The new, smaller population would then differ from the larger population that it came from.

However, there is a theory regarding populations which do not evolve. **The Hardy-Weinberg Theorem** states that the frequencies of alleles and genotypes in a population's gene pool remain constant through the generations, unless some outside force impacts the gene pool. In these cases, random fertilization and the shuffling of alleles have no impact on the overall gene pool. According to Hardy-Weinberg, five conditions must be met in order for a population to remain in equilibrium.

1. A large population size. In small populations, fluctuations in the gene pool would cause random changes in genotype called **genetic drift**.

2. No gene flow or transfer of alleles due to migration.

3. No mutations.

4. Random mating. If individuals were to mate based on particular genotypes, then the mixing of the gene pool would not be random.

5. No natural selection.

These conditions rarely exist in nature for any amount of time.

Evidence for Evolutionary Change

The fossil record provides evidence that organisms have evolved through time; some have gone extinct, and others have not changed very much at all. Comparative embryology shows us that, during the early stages of development, distantly-related organisms possess some similar structures – this provides evidence of a common ancestry.

We can also see some structures in the adult stages of distantly-related organisms that may appear different, but actually developed from the same original structure. These are referred to as **homologous structures**.

Vestigial structures are "leftovers" that do not serve a purpose today. Some examples of human vestigial structures are the appendix, coccyx (tail bone), and *plica luminaris* (protective component of the eye).

The entire idea of natural selection is based on the idea that organisms adapt to their particular environment. When the environment changes, those individuals better adapted to the environment will survive. This results in evolution.

Evolution in organisms can take place in a number of ways.

In **convergent evolution**, two (or more) distantly-related species may evolve similar behaviors and/or appearances because they are adapting to a similar environment.

In **coevolution**, two species may evolve characteristics because of the close association between them. The changes are a direct result of the interactions.

Divergent evolution occurs when two or more species have an original common ancestor and are closely related. When those species eventually diverge, they evolve completely different traits and characteristics due to a need to adapt to different environments and conditions.

> **Adaptive radiation**, where two or more species develop from a common ancestor but evolve differing traits due to different habitats, is a form of divergent evolution.

In fact, life as we know it depends upon the idea of evolution. There, several major developments had to have taken place.

- The formation of simple organic molecules. It is possible that these molecules developed in Earth's early atmosphere and were then carried into the oceans.

- Self-replication of the molecules would have been the next major development. As the genetic material within the molecules was copied and passed on, natural selection would begin to take place.

- Next, the self-replicating molecules would become enclosed in a cell membrane.

- A pivotal development: The evolution of modern metabolic processes and the ability for those cells to out-compete other organisms.

Knowing this, we can note that, approximately two-billion years ago, multi-cellular organisms evolved, and cells evolved specialized functions. Following that:

- The first vertebrates with true bones appeared approximately 485 million years ago.

- 434 million years ago, primitive plants moved onto land.

- Amphibians gave rise to reptiles approximately 305 million years ago.

- The earliest dinosaurs and first mammals appeared 225 million years ago.

- The first hominine appeared 6.5 million years ago.

- Two-million years ago: The first of the genus Homo appears.

The **principle of punctuated equilibrium** states that species living in stable environments do not have a large degree of evolutionary changes. It is only when the existing environment changes suddenly, or the species moves to a new environment, that selective pressures may force sudden evolutionary change and speciation.

On the other end of evolution lies extinction. **Extinction** occurs when a species does not evolve to adapt to new environmental conditions. If the species does not possess the traits it needs to survive, then it will go extinct and die out.

Organisms and the Environment

One of the most basic differences between organisms is the distinction between prokaryotes and eukaryotes. **Prokaryotes** are the most primitive form of single-celled organisms – generally bacteria. They lack a nucleus to hold their genetic material, so their DNA is simply bundled within the cell.

Eukaryotes are the more advanced cells. They can be very complex, and contain multiple organelles within them. These **organelles** perform specialized functions within the cell. Eukaryotes, being more complex, are larger than prokaryotes.

Another basic way to compare, or classify, organisms is via their methods of obtaining energy. For plants, this is done through photosynthesis. Other organisms break down organic matter.

CLASSIFICATION OF ORGANISMS

All of Earth's organisms have characteristics which distinguish them from one another. Scientists have developed systems to organize and classify all of Earth's organisms based on those characteristics.

Kingdoms

Through the process of evolution, organisms on Earth have developed into many diverse forms, which have complex relationships. Scientists have organized life into five large groups called **kingdoms**.

Each kingdom contains those organisms that share significant characteristics distinguishing them from organisms in other kingdoms. These five kingdoms are named as follows:

1. **Animalia**.
2. **Plantae**.
3. **Fungi**.
4. **Protista**.
5. **Monera**.

Kingdom Animalia
This kingdom contains multicellular organisms multicellular, or those known as complex organisms. These organisms are generically called **heterotrophs**, which means that they must eat preexisting organic matter (either plants or other animals) in order to sustain themselves.

Those heterotrophs which eat only plants are called **herbivores** (from "herbo," meaning "herb" or "plant"); those that kill and eat other animals for food are called **carnivores** (from "carno," meaning "flesh" or "meat"); and still other animals eat both plants *and* other animals – they are called **omnivores** (from "omnis," which means "all").

Those organisms in the Animal Kingdom have nervous tissue which has developed into nervous systems and brains; they are also able to move from place to place using muscular systems. The Animal Kingdom is divided into two groups: **vertebrates** (with backbones) and **invertebrates** (without backbones).

Kingdom Plantae
As you can guess from its name, the Plant Kingdom contains all plant-based life. Plants are multicellular organisms that use chlorophyll, which is held in specialized cellular structures called **chloroplasts,** to capture sunlight energy. Remember: photosynthesis! They then convert that sunlight energy into organic matter: their food. Because of this,

most plants are referred to as **autotrophs** (self-feeders). There are a few organisms included in the Plant Kingdom which are not multicellular – certain types of algae which, while not multicellular, have cells with a nucleus. These algae also contain chlorophyll.

Except for algae, most plants are divided into one of two groups: **vascular plants** (most crops, trees, and flowering plants) and **nonvascular plants** (mosses). Vascular plants have specialized tissue that allows them to transport water and nutrients from their roots, to their leaves, and back again – even when the plant is several hundred feet tall. Nonvascular plants cannot do this, and therefore remain very small in size. Vascular plants are able to grow in both wet and dry environments; whereas nonvascular plants, since they are unable to transport water, are usually found only in wet, marshy areas.

Kingdom Fungi

The Fungi Kingdom contains organisms that share some similarities with plants, but also have other characteristics that make them more animal-like. For example, they resemble animals in that they lack chlorophyll – so they can't perform photosynthesis. This means that they don't produce their own food and are therefore heterotrophs.

However, they resemble plants in that they reproduce by spores; they also resemble plants in appearance. The bodies of fungi are made of filaments called **hyphae**, which in turn create the tissue **mycelium.** The most well-known examples of organisms in this Kingdom are mushrooms, yeasts, and molds. Fungi are very common and benefit other organisms, including humans.

Kingdom Protista

This kingdom includes single-celled organisms that contain a nucleus as part of their structure. They are considered a simple cell, but still contain multiple structures and accomplish many functions. This Kingdom includes organisms such as paramecium, amoeba, and slime molds. They often move around using hair-like structures called *cilia* or *flagellums.*

Kingdom Monera

This kingdom contains only bacteria. All of these organisms are single-celled and do not have a nucleus. They have only one chromosome, which is used to transfer genetic information. Sometimes they can also transmit genetic information using small structures called **plasmids.** Like organisms in the Protista Kingdom, they use flagella to move. Bacteria usually reproduce asexually.

There are more forms of bacteria than any other organism on Earth. Some bacteria are beneficial to us, like the ones found in yogurt; others can cause us to get sick such as the bacteria *E. coli.*

KINGDOM	DESCRIPTION	EXAMPLES
Animalia	Multi-celled; parasites; prey; consumers; can be herbivorous, carnivorous, or omnivorous	Sponges, worms, insects, fish, mammals, reptiles, birds, humans
Plantae	Multi-celled; autotrophs; mostly producers	Ferns, angiosperms, gymnosperms, mosses
Fungi	Can be single or multi-celled; decomposers; parasites; absorb food; asexual; consumers	Mushrooms, mildew, molds, yeast
Protista	Single or multi-celled; absorb food; both producers and consumers	Plankton, algae, amoeba, protozoans
Monera	Single-celled or a colony of single-cells; decomposers and parasites; move in water; are both producers and consumers	Bacteria, blue-green algae

Levels of Classification

Kingdom groupings are not very specific. They contain organisms defined by broad characteristics, and which may not seem similar at all. For example, worms belong in Kingdom Animalia – but then, so do birds. These two organisms are very different, despite sharing the necessary traits to make it into the animal kingdom. Therefore, to further distinguish different organisms, we have multiple levels of classification, which gradually become more specific until we finally reach the actual organism.

We generally start out by grouping organisms into the appropriate kingdom. Within each kingdom, we have other subdivisions: **Phylum, Class, Order, Family, Genus, and Species.** (In some cases, "Species" can be further narrowed down into "Sub-Species.")

As we move down the chain, characteristics become more specific, and the number of organisms in each group decreases. For an example, let's try to classify a grizzly bear. The chart would go as follows:

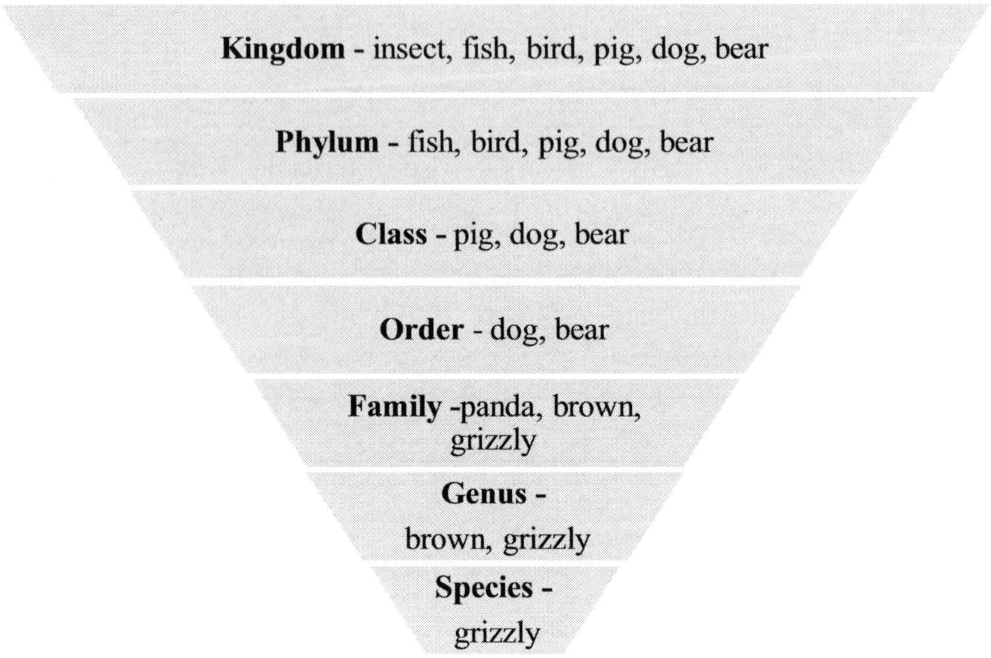

Here is an easy way to remember the order of terms used in this classification scheme:

Kings **P**lay **C**ards **O**n **F**riday, **G**enerally **S**peaking.
Kingdom, **P**hylum, **C**lass, **O**rder, **F**amily, **G**enus, **S**pecies

Binomial Nomenclature

Organisms can be positively identified by two Latin words. Therefore, the organism naming system is referred to as a binomial nomenclature ("binomial" referring to the number two, and "nomenclature" referring to a title or name). Previously-used words help illustrate where the organism fits into the whole scheme, but it is only the last two, the genus and species, that specifically name an organism. Both are written in italics. The genus is always capitalized, but the species name is written lowercase.

Grizzly bears fall underneath the genus *Ursus*, species *arctos*, and sub-species *horribilis*. Therefore, the scientific name of the grizzly bear would be *Ursus arctos horribilis. Canis familiaris* is the scientific name for a common dog, *Felis domesticus* is a common cat, and humans are *Homo sapiens*.

MICROORGANISMS

Microorganisms (microbes) are extremely small and cannot be seen with the naked eye. They can be detected using either a microscope or through various chemical tests. These organisms are everywhere, even in such extreme environments as very hot areas, very cold areas, dry areas, and deep in the ocean under tremendous pressure. Some of these organisms cause diseases in animals, plants, and humans. However, most are helpful to us and the Earth's ecosystems. In fact, we are totally dependent upon microbes for our quality of life. There are three types of microorganisms: **bacteria, protists, and fungi.**

Bacteria

Bacteria are microorganisms that do not have a true nucleus; their genetic material simply floats around in the cell. They are very small, simple, one-celled organisms. Bacteria are normally found in three variations: **bacilli** (rod-shaped), **cocci** (sphere-shaped), and **spirilla** (spiral-shaped). Bacteria are widespread in all environments and are important participants within all ecosystems. They are **decomposers**, because they break down dead organic matter into basic molecules.

Bacteria are also an important part of the food-chain, because they are eaten by other organisms. Still, bacteria remain the most numerous organisms on Earth. This is due to the fact that they are small, can live practically anywhere, and have great metabolic flexibility. But most importantly, bacteria have the ability to rapidly reproduce. In the right environment, any bacteria can reproduce every 20 or 30 minutes, each one doubling after each reproduction.

Benefits of Bacteria – Some bacteria are found in our intestinal tracts, where they help to digest our food and make vitamins.

To demonstrate the significance of bacteria, let's look at the cycle of nitrogen, which is used by organisms to make proteins. The cycle starts with dead plants being decomposed by bacteria. The nitrogen from the plant tissue is released into the atmosphere, where nitrifying bacteria convert that nitrogen into ammonia-type compounds. Other bacteria act upon these compounds to form nitrates for plants to absorb. When these new plants die, we are brought back again to the decomposing bacteria releasing the plant's nitrogen into the atmosphere.

Bacterial Diseases - Microorganisms, including bacteria, enter our bodies in a variety of ways: through the air we breathe, ingestion by mouth, or through the skin via a cut or injury. We can eliminate much of this threat by disinfecting utensils and thoroughly washing our hands. This destroys bacteria and other microorganisms which may cause disease.

Protists

Protists are very diversified and include organisms that range greatly in size – from single cells to considerably complex structures, some longer than 100 meters. Protists have a wide variety of reproductive and nutritional strategies, and their genetic material is enclosed within a nucleus. Even though protists are more simplistic than other organisms with cellular nuclei, they are not as primitive as bacteria.

Some are autotrophic and contain chlorophyll; others are heterotrophic and consume other organisms to survive. Because protists obtain food in both of these ways, it is generally believed that early protists were both animal- and plant-like. Protists are important to food chains and ecosystems, although some protists do cause disease.

Fungi

Fungi are heterotrophic and can be either single-celled or multi-celled. They play an important decomposition role in an ecosystem, because they consume dead organic matter. This returns nutrients to the soil for eventual uptake by plants.

There are three types of fungi which obtain food: saprophytic, parasitic, and mycorrhizal-associated.

Saprophytic fungi consume dead organic matter; **parasitic** fungi attack living plants and animals; and **mycorrhizal-associated** fungi form close relationships (**symbiosis**) with trees, shrubs, and other plants, where each partner in the relationship mutually benefits. An organism called **lichen** is an example of a symbiotic union between a fungus and algae.

Fungi produce **spores** (reproductive structures) that are highly resistant to extreme temperatures and moisture levels. This gives them the ability to survive for a long time, even in aggressive environments. When their environments become more favorable, the spores **germinate** (sprout) and grow. Spores are able to travel to new areas, which spreads the organism. Fungi absorb food through **hyphae**. A large mass of joined, branched hyphae is called the **mycelium**, which constitutes the main body of the multicellular fungi. However, the mycelium is not usually seen, because it is hidden throughout the food source which is being consumed. The largest organism in the world is believed to be a soil fungus whose mycelium tissue extends for many acres!

What we do usually see of a fungus is the fungal fruiting body. A mushroom is a fruiting body filled with spores. The main body of the mushroom (the **mycelium**) is under the soil surface.

ECOLOGY

Biosphere and Biome

Life is possible due to the presence of air (**atmosphere**), water (**hydrosphere**), and soil (**lithosphere**). These factors interact with each other and the life on Earth to create an environment called a **biosphere**. The biosphere contains all of Earth's living organisms. Smaller living systems called **biomes** exist in large areas, both on land and in water; they are defined by the physical characteristics of the environment which they encompass, and by the organisms living within it.

Ecosystem

An ecosystem is a community of living and non-living things that work together. Ecosystems have no particular size; from large lakes and deserts, to small trees or puddles. Everything in the natural world – water, water temperature, plants, animals, air, light, soil, etc. – all form ecosystems.

The physical environment of an ecosystem includes soils, weather, climate, the topography (or shape) of the land, and many other factors. If there isn't enough light or water within an ecosystem, or if the soil doesn't have the right nutrients, plants will die. If plants die, the animals which depend on them will die. If the animals depending upon the plants die, any other animals depending upon those animals will also die. Regardless of the type of ecosystem they are in, all organisms – even microscopic ones – are affected by each other and their physical surroundings.

There are two components of an ecosystem. The **biotic** (biological) component includes the living organisms; nonliving factors – such as water, minerals, and sunlight – are collectively known as the **abiotic** (non-biological) component.

While all ecosystems have different organisms and/or abiotic factors, they all have two primary features:

1. **Energy flows in one direction**. Beginning in the form of chemical bonds from photosynthetic organisms, like green plants or algae, energy flows first to the animals that eat the plants, then to other animals.

2. **Inorganic materials are recycled**. When taken up from the environment through living organisms, inorganic minerals are returned to the environment – mainly via decomposers such as bacteria and fungi. Other organisms called **detritivores** (such as pill bugs, sow bugs, millipedes, and earthworms), help break down large pieces of organic matter into smaller pieces that are handled then by the decomposers.

But since that's a lot of information to take in at once, here's a simple and complete definition of an ecosystem: a combination of biotic and abiotic components, through which energy flows and inorganic material is recycled.

An Organism's Niche

The area in which an organism lives – and therefore acquires the many things needed to sustain their lives – is called a **habitat.** An organism's role within its community, how it affects its habitat and how it is affected by its habitat, are the factors that define the organism's **niche**. A niche is like an organism's "location" and "occupation" within a community. For example, birds and squirrels both live in a tree habitat; however, they eat different foods, have different living arrangements, and have different food-gathering abilities. Therefore, the do not occupy the same niche.

THE ECOLOGICAL ORDER OF LIFE

Biosphere – All ecosystems on the planet make up the biosphere.

Ecosystem – Large community of numerous communities, and the physical non-living environment.

Community – A group of populations in a given area.

Population – A group of organisms of the same species in a given area.

Organism – A living thing.

Organ Systems – A group of organs that perform certain functions to form an organism.

Organs – A group of tissues that perform a certain function to form organ systems.

Tissues – A group of cells that perform certain functions to form an organ.

Cells – The building blocks of life that form tissues.

Organelles – Small parts of cells that have specific functions.

Atoms and Molecules – The building blocks of everything in the known universe.

One of the most important relationships among organisms exists between predators and their prey. You may have heard of this relationship described through **food chains** and **food webs**.

Food Chains represent the flow of energy obtained from the chemical breakdown of food molecules. When one animal (the predator) consumes another (the prey), the chemical bonds making up the tissues of the prey's body are broken down by the predator's digestive system. This digestive process releases energy and smaller chemical molecules that the predator's body uses to make more tissue. Prior to being the consumed, the prey obtains energy from foods for its own life processes.

Here's a basic example of a food chain:

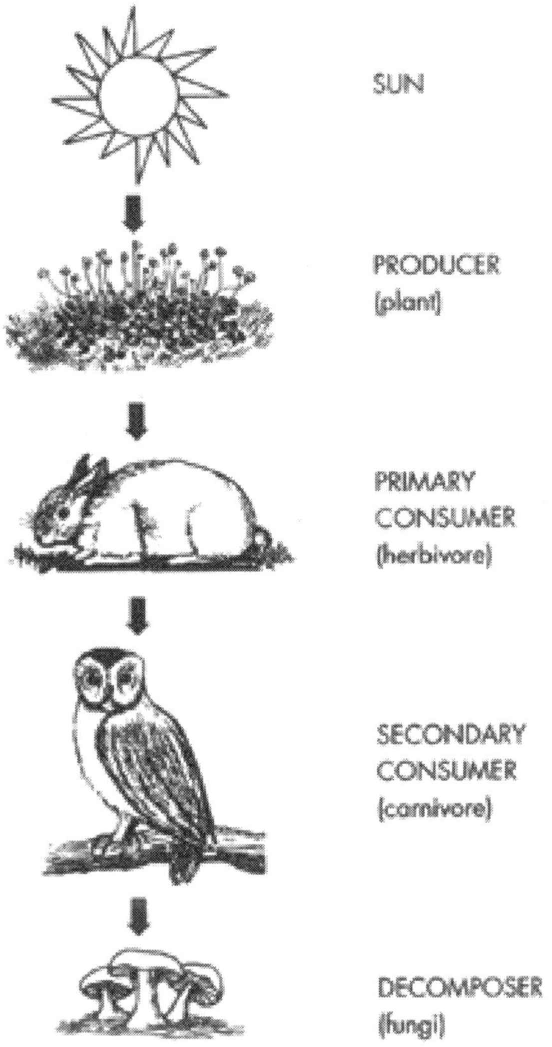

[2]

Food chains are a part of **food webs**, which offer a more complex view of energy transfer. They include more organisms, taking into account more than one predator-prey relationship. Each step along a food chain, or within a food web, is called a **trophic** (or feeding) level. Organisms at that first trophic level are known as **primary producers**, and are always photosynthetic organisms, whether on land or in water.

At the second trophic level, herbivores (referred to as **primary consumers**) eat plants to produce the energy needed for their metabolism. Much of the energy that transfers from the first trophic level to the second level is not turned into tissue. Instead, it is used for the digestive process, locomotion, and is lost as heat. As you move from one trophic level to another, it is estimated that only 10% of the available energy gets turned into body tissue at the next level up.
The following is an example of a food web:

[2] Graphic from: http://www.king.portlandschools.org

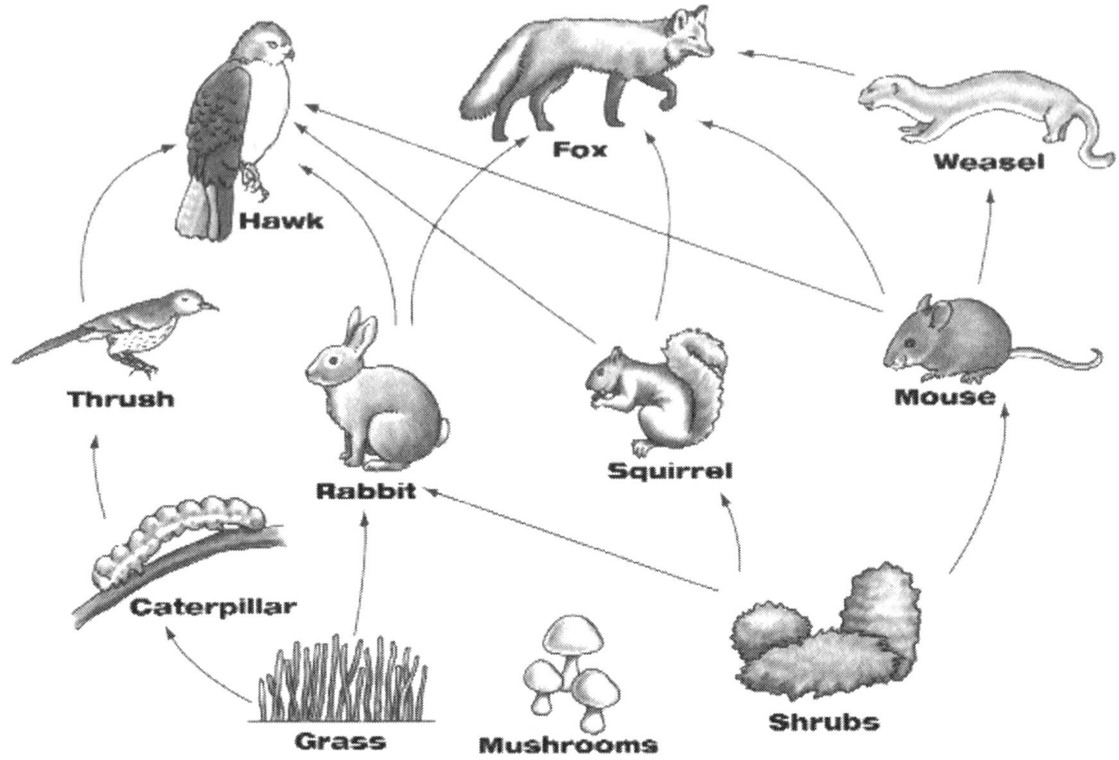

[3]

Ecosystems experience change constantly, sometimes gradually, sometimes rapidly. **Succession** is the term for the changes that occur within a community of an ecosystem. In **primary succession**, a new community develops where there were no previous organisms present.

> An example of this would be a community developing on a cooled lava flow. New species may rapidly occupy the area. When the community becomes stable, it is called the **climax community**. However it is now believed that ecosystems never reach a point where they stop changing. They remain dynamic, and new communities may overlap. As succession occurs, different plants and animals with different niche requirements may adapt.

When human activity or natural disasters partially destroy a community, **secondary succession** can occur. In this case, species that were not part of the original community replace the originals. Biodiversity plays an important role in ecosystem stability. The more biological diversity there is in a community, the more stable and productive the community is. An example of a monoculture that lacks biodiversity is an agricultural field. When one type of plant is present, it is susceptible to failure and there would be nothing left.

---

[3] Graphic from: http://www.education.com

Primary succession and secondary succession are two ways new environments are created. Primary succession is when naturally desolate land is transformed into life-sustaining land. Secondary succession is when a functioning ecosystem must redevelop after a disruption (such as a fire or flood).

Test Your Knowledge

1. Ecology is the study of organisms interacting with:
   a) The physical environment only.
   b) The internal environment only.
   c) The physical environment and each other.
   d) Each other and the internal environment.

2. In terms of energy, an ecosystem is defined as:
   a) Moving energy back and forth between organisms.
   b) Moving energy in one direction from plants to animals.
   c) Not utilizing energy.
   d) Moving energy in one direction from animals to plants.

3. Decomposers are important because they:
   a) Recycle nutrients.
   b) Produce sugars.
   c) Produce oxygen.
   d) Engage in asexual reproduction.

4. Which of the following best describes the concept of an organism's niche?
   a) It is the organism's function, or "occupation", within an ecosystem.
   b) It is the organism's location, or "address", within an ecosystem.
   c) It is both an organism's function and location in an ecosystem.
   d) It is the binomial classification of an organism in an ecosystem.

5. The steps in a food chain or food web are called ______ and represent the _______of an organism.
   a) biome levels; energy level
   b) trophic levels; energy level
   c) trophic levels; feeding level
   d) energy levels; feeding level

6. Another term for herbivores is:
   a) Plants.
   b) Secondary consumers.
   c) Primary consumers
   d) Third trophic-level organisms.

7. Several interacting food chains form a:
   a) Food pyramid.
   b) Food web.
   c) Food column.
   d) Food triangle.

8. Herbivores are at the second trophic level, so they are:

a) Primary producers.
b) Primary consumers.
c) Secondary consumers.
d) Secondary producers.

Test Your Knowledge – Answers

1. c)
2. b)
3. a)
4. c)
5. c)
6. c)
7. b)
8. b)

Chapter 4: Diversity of Life, Plants, & Animals

Learning about the diversity of life is the basis of the study of biological sciences. Knowledge of this area will be beneficial no matter what branch of science is being taught.

Nature of Science

Plants and animals inhabit various aquatic and terrestrial environments all across the world. Some climate conditions in these environments are extreme, result in special **adaptations** among the plants and animals who survive there. The chart below compares and contrasts **structural** and **physiological** adaptations in various biomes.

Biome	Plant Adaptation(s)	Animal Adaptation(s)
Freshwater	Most plants have adapted to living in the wide parts of rivers and streams which allows more sunlight.	Most land animals feed off the abundance of fish and insects that live in the freshwater. Many have found warm parts of the biome, which eliminates the need to migrate.
Marine	Some plants can grow as deep as 100 feet below the water's surface and provide homes for many sea creatures.	Fish have gills that allow them to breathe under water, fins and sleek bodies allowing them to swim through the water, and eyes on the sides of their heads to see predators.
Forest	The trees lean toward the sun to acquire more sunlight and can pull nutrients from deep underground.	The animals migrate during the winter and use the trees for food, water, and shelter.
Plain	Trees have tough trunks and deep roots to withstand potential fires. Grasses have soft stems that allow them to blow in the wind.	Many animals have limbs that allow them to move very quickly, and they can also burrow to escape the wind.
Desert	Plants have shallow roots and lack leaves to retain more water. Photosynthesis occurs in the stem.	Animals are only active at night when it's cooler and most have large ears to give off more heat.
Tundra	Plants grow close to the ground and close to each other to keep from freezing. They have shallow roots to penetrate ice.	Animals have two layers of fur and blubber to keep them warmer. They migrate during the harsher winters.

Most ecosystems experience climate changes. Some of these changes are more extreme than others. Animals have two options when it comes to responding to such changes: **adapt** or **migrate**. Some animals are able to withstand climate changes by having certain biological adaptations, or by hibernating to store energy. Other animals choose to migrate to areas with a more favorable climate, returning when the climate regains its suitability. If animals are not able to adapt or migrate, they risk dying or extinction.

A **classification scheme** is descriptive information that is used to place organisms into groups based on shared characteristics. They are used to better study organisms. It also helps to identify unknown organisms by suggesting other related organisms. These schemes are beneficial, but they also have limitations. The most explicit limitation is the fact that descriptive information could be subjective and based solely on the opinion of the observer. This discrepancy in opinion could cause the same organism to be grouped differently by different people.

Taxonomic classification refers to the organization of organisms in such a way that depicts relationships. This type of classification is helpful in that it not only shows how organisms are related, but it also shows how an organism has evolved over time. Taxonomic classification gives an **evolutionary** history of an organism's development.

> When classifying organisms by way of taxonomy, there are some types of traits that are more useful than others.
>
> **Homologous traits,** which refer to the same traits found in different organisms, are helpful in depicting relationships among organisms. This is because these traits are only homologous if they were inherited from a common ancestor.
>
> On the other hand, **convergent traits** are not used in taxonomy. Convergent traits are those that are developed by organisms independently. This means the trait did not come from a common ancestor and can therefore not be used to prove ancestral relationships. For example, insects and birds both have wings that allow them to fly, but this not constitute proof of them being ancestors of one another.

A **hierarchical classification** system contains different levels. Each level can be analyzed for relationships among the organisms on that level. These relationships are then used to form a system for classifying and identifying organisms. A **dichotomous key** classifies and identifies all aquatic and terrestrial organisms.

The broadest level of classification for organisms is the Kingdom. The dichotomous key can be used to classify organisms to their Phylum, Class, Order, Family, Genus, and Species based on the identification of certain traits.

All organisms are grouped within three **domains**: Bacteria, Archaea, and Eukarya. Within each domain, organisms are further divided into six **kingdoms**. This grouping is based on distinguishing characteristics only shared by organisms within each domain and kingdom.

Though we've already reviewed such classification in our chapter over Heredity and Evolution of Life, look at the chart below to see key characteristics for organisms within each domain and kingdom.

Domain	Associated Kingdom(s)	Key Characteristics	Examples
Bacteria	Bacteria	"True bacteria." Prokaryotes. Contain no nucleus.	Salmonella, E. Coli
Archaea	Archaea	"Ancient bacteria." Prokaryotes. Contain no nucleus. Cell wall structure and other chemicals differ from bacteria.	Halophiles, methanogens
Eukarya	Protista, Fungi, Plantae, Animalia	DNA in chromosomes. Cells contain organelles.	Trees, amoeba, mushrooms, mammals

Boundaries and Limits of Living Systems

There are five basic needs that are necessary for organisms to carry out life functions:

1. **Nutrients** or food provide organisms with the energy needed to carry out all basic survival functions. Some organisms make their own food, while others rely on other organisms for food.

2. In order to use the energy that is obtained from food, something must release the energy. **Oxygen** combines with food to release its energy in order for the organism to utilize it.

3. **Water** is essential for proper cell function. It helps dissolve food as well as waste. Water makes up 70% of the cell.

4. **Carbon dioxide** is the waste product given off by most animals once they have used oxygen to gain energy. Plants use carbon dioxide to make their own food, and thus supply animals with oxygen. Without carbon dioxide, plants would not survive and therefore would not be able to serve as an oxygen supply.

5. A **space** to live that will provide an organism with all of its necessities is vital to survival. If an organism does not have access to all of the resources needed to live, it will not survive.

Different types of organisms have their own methods for making sure their energy needs are met.

Animals and humans obtain their energy from the foods that they consume. They also take in oxygen, which then combines with food during digestion to release its energy into the body. The energy is then stored in the muscles as ATP. This energy is released only when it is needed by the body to perform work. Plants absorb energy directly from the sun, using photosynthesis to make sugar and starches which store the absorbed energy. This energy is released once the plant is eaten by an animal, or once the plant dies and begins to decay.

Some bacteria feed off of decaying organisms. Once a dead organism begins to decay, it releases its stored energy. As bacteria break down the organism, they gain that energy. Other bacteria have the ability to make their own energy. Both groups of bacteria then release acquired energy back into the environment.

Homeostasis

There are 11 basic body or organ systems that help keep the body in homeostasis. Many of these body systems works together in order to keep the body functioning properly. The following chart summarizes these body systems.

Body System	Main Organs	Function
Digestive	Stomach and intestines.	Breaks down food to a usable form.
Circulatory	Heart and blood vessels.	Transports blood throughout the body delivering nutrients and removing waste.
Nervous	Brain, spinal cord, and nerves.	Send and receive messages throughout the body.
Endocrine	Glands such as the thyroid and pituitary.	Releases hormones necessary for various bodily functions.
Reproductive	Uterus, penis, ovaries, and testes.	Responsible for enabling an organism to produce new life.
Integumentary	Skin.	Outer covering of the body that provides the first layer of defense.
Skeletal	Bones.	Supports the body and gives it shape while also protecting vital organs.
Respiratory	Lungs, trachea, and diaphragm.	Brings oxygen into the body and releases carbon dioxide out of the body.
Muscular	Muscles.	Controls movement within the body.
Excretory	Bladder, kidneys, ureters, and urethra.	Rids the body of waste.
Immune	Spleen, lymph nodes, and thymus gland.	Protects the body against disease and other illnesses.

Although plants do not contain organ systems, they do possess systems that help regulate their daily functions.

The following chart summarizes plant systems.

System	Plant Part(s)	Function
Transport System	Xylem and phloem.	Used to transport water, sugar and other nutrients throughout the plant.
Control System	Nuclei of plant cells.	Controls function of each plant part.
Reproductive System	Flower, stamen, and carpel.	Allows plants to multiply.
Nutritional System	Roots and leaves.	Allows the plant to acquire water, energy, and other nutrients needed for daily functions.
Structural System	Various plant tissue.	Used to support, protect, prevent water loss, and store food in plants.

Plants have two methods of **reproduction** – **asexual** and **sexual**. Many parts of a plant can be sites for asexual reproduction. A plant cell copies its DNA and then divides thus beginning the growth of a new plant. This can happen almost anywhere on a plant.

Only one plant is needed for asexual reproduction and the offspring plant is identical to the parent in every way. During sexual reproduction, the nucleus of a male plant gamete joins the nucleus of a female plant gamete.

Most plants have both female and male parts. Once the two gametes fuse, the cell multiplies and becomes a new plant sharing genetic information with both parent plants.

Most animals reproduce through sexual reproduction. There are a few that use an asexual method. During animal sexual reproduction, a female egg must be fertilized by a male sperm. Each sex cell (sperm and egg) brings genetic information from the parent. The offspring is then a combination of traits from both parents. Once the cell is fertilized, it begins to multiply and grow into an offspring.

Remember, **homeostasis** is the process by which an organism maintains a stable, internal environment. Stability in this sense means to be in equilibrium. If the organisms' **internal environment** does not remain in equilibrium, normal bodily functions will not be able to take place. Most bodily functions are vital to the survival of an organism so if they cease, the organism may not be able to survive.

The body has internal **feedback** systems that help regulate its internal environment. These systems are known as positive or negative feedback systems and alert a response from the body when a condition is not in a homeostatic state. For example, when an animal gets cut and is bleeding, the body's feedback systems cause the body's reaction to form a clot to stop the bleeding.

If feedback systems were not in place, the organism could not maintain equilibrium of proper blood circulation and bleed to death.

There are anatomical structures and physiological processes within organisms that function to maintain homeostasis in the face of changing environmental conditions.

- **Negative feedback** – if an activity within the body of an animal is hyperactive, negative feedback slows down the activity to return the body to a normal state. For example, if the body is being deprived of food, the body will slow down metabolic action in an effort to conserve nutrients.

- **Positive feedback** – if an activity within the body of an animal needs to increase, positive feedback will accelerate the activity in order to return the body to a homeostatic environment. The blood clotting scenario mentioned previously is an example of positive feedback.

- **Turgor pressure** – in plants, turgor pressure is used to regulate the water flow in plants. If a plant is wilting, it is because there is not enough water flowing through the stem of the plant. The plant can then increase turgor pressure in order to keep water flow at a normal rate. This is an example of negative feedback in plants.

Being in a homeostatic state is only the beginning of necessary condition that an organism needs to survive. In order for the body systems to perform and keep the body in homeostasis, there are a few other conditions that must be met.

- The body requires proper **nutrition** in order to function well. Food and nutrients are what provides the body with the energy to perform. If the body lacks nutrients, body systems will not be able to keep the body in the correct state of equilibrium.

- Proper **environmental conditions** must also be met. These conditions include where an organism lives. The environment must have the necessary resources for survival such as water, food, and even shelter. An organism has to be able to protect its body from extreme climate conditions so that the body can perform appropriately.

- **Exercise** provides many health benefits to an organism. It strengthens muscles, provides the body with additional energy, and reduces extra fat stored by the body. These benefits provide a good internal environment for the body systems to perform.

Viruses and other microorganisms such as bacteria have both positive and negative effects on the homeostasis in organisms.**Viruses** can disrupt homeostasis when introduced into the body. When a virus enters the body, it immediately looks for cells on which to attach. The only way a virus can survive and multiply is by attaching to a cell and taking over its functions.

Once a virus starts taking over cells in the body, normal body functions slow down until the virus is illuminated. Sometimes the virus can prove to be very dangerous if not controlled. A virus can cause body functions to cease all together.

On the other hand, some microorganisms such as bacteria assist the body with homeostasis. There are **bacteria** in the intestines of humans and animals that help break down food during the digestion process. This process of breaking down food is important in keeping the body in homeostasis.

Biology and Behavior

The **behavior** of organisms, including humans, is in response to internal or external stimuli. This response is controlled by the nervous and endocrine systems in humans. Behavior refers to any action that takes place whether internally or externally and whether voluntary or involuntary.

> An example of an involuntary behavior would be breathing when your body requires more oxygen and blinking when our eyes are dry. These are behaviors that the body performs on its own when triggered internally.

Some behaviors (like breathing and blinking) are innate while others (such as walking) are **learned**. Some behaviors are even thought to be **genetic**. Instincts for example are behaviors that are thought to be inherited and are species specific. Mental illness can also be an inherited behavior. Other behaviors require a combination of genetics and learned factors. For example, babies are born with the ability to move their limbs but they must learn how to control those movements.

Innate and learned patterns of behavior do have their adaptive advantages. These behaviors are necessary for survival and reproduction. The innate ability of a baby knowing how to suck is essential for its survival because this is how he/she will primarily eat for several months. The baby can adapt to not only feed from a breast but also a bottle with a nipple. Predators learned behavior of hunting prey is an adaptive measure taken for the animal to survive in any environment that provides the appropriate prey.

There are some innate and learned factors that help to mediate certain behaviors. **Imprinting** has been observed in animals, insects, and plants. It is a natural process by which certain genes, although present, are "turned-off" or not expressed in an offspring. Sometimes the behavioral effects are positive and other times, the behavioral effect comes in the form of disease.

Hormonal systems within the body regulate body development. When certain hormones are being released or have stopped being released, the effects can be seen in the organism's behavior. When a child goes through hormonal changes, his/her entire attitude and mannerisms could change. Learned behaviors such as **playing** and **classical conditioning** can change behavior. Rewarding an animal for proper behavior and punishing for misbehavior can train the animal to behave appropriately.

There are theories that suggest that natural selection occurs in favor of organisms who exhibit favorable behavior. Kin selection falls in line with such theories. With **kin selection**, organisms are favored based on the behaviors of their ancestors. A worker ant is born a worker ant because his ancestors were worker ants.

Altruistic behavior also stems from kin selection. Animals act according to those before them. **Courtship behavior** in animals also suggests this theory of natural selection. Proper courtship behavior allows a species of animal to reproduce with the same species that shares similar qualities.

Test Your Knowledge: Diversity of Life

1. True/False: You would most likely find very tall trees in the desert biome because of all the sunlight they receive.

2. True/False: Taxonomic classification gives the evolutionary history of an organism.

3. True/False: Homologous traits are those developed independently by organisms.

4. What is the difference between a domain and a kingdom?

5. What are the five basic needs of living organisms?

6. How do animals meet their energy needs?
   a) Taking vitamins.
   b) Exercising.
   c) Eating plants.
   d) Absorbing it from the sun.

7. Skin is the main organ of which body system?
   a) Integumentary.
   b) Muscular.
   c) Skeletal.
   d) Immune.

8. Which body system releases hormones to keep the body in homeostasis?
   a) Immune.
   b) Endocrine.
   c) Nervous.
   d) Circulatory.

9. Which type of feedback system accelerates an activity to restore homeostasis?

10. Which two body systems control the behavior of an organism?

11. Decide if the following is an innate trait or learned behavior: *Spine of a cactus.*

12. Decide if the following is an innate trait or learned behavior: *Reading quickly.*

13. Decide if the following is an innate trait or learned behavior: *Speaking with an accent.*

Test Your Knowledge: Diversity of Life – Answers

1. **False**.
Although there is much sunlight in the desert biome, trees tend to be shorter. (Remember, plants in the desert have shallow roots, lack leaves to retain water, and have short growth cycles.)

2. **True**.

3. **False**.
Homologous traits are those inherited from a common ancestor.

4. **A domain is more general than a kingdom**. **A kingdom is a more detailed way to further divide a domain**.

5. **Nutrients**, **oxygen**, **water**, **carbon dioxide**, and **space**.

6. **c)**
They can also eat plant-eating animals.

7. **a)**

8. **b)**

9. **Positive feedback**.

10. **Nervous** and **endocrine**.

11. **Innate trait**.

12. **Learned behavior**.

13. **Learned behavior**.

Additional Biology Practice Questions

1. Which of the following is responsible for the hydrolysis of acetylcholine into acetic acid choline?
    a. Acetylcholine
    b. Cholinesterase
    c. Dopamine
    d. Serotonin

2. Which of the following structures are found in eukaryotes and not prokaryotes?
    a. DNA and mitochondria
    b. Chloroplasts and flagella
    c. Ribosomes and Golgi complex
    d. Mitochondria and endoplasmic reticulum

3. Which of the following is a function of free ribosomes?
    a. Assemble amino acids into protein.
    b. Break down food and cellular debris.
    c. Serves as the site for DNA replication.
    d. Serves as the site for aerobic respiration.

4. Which of the following would be produced in mRNA if a transcription of the DNA is CCGGAAAT?
    a. GGCCTTTA
    b. CCGGAAAT
    c. UUAACCCA
    d. GGCCUUUA

5. The ripening of fruit is promoted by:
    a. Carotenes
    b. Abscisic acid
    c. Ethylene
    d. Gibberellins

6. When water moves out of a cell causing the cell to collapse, this is referred to as:
    a. Plasmolysis
    b. Exocytosis
    c. Dialysis
    d. Endocytosis

7. Which of the following has a body plan with bilateral symmetry?
    a. Hydrozoans
    b. Jellyfish
    c. Flatworms
    d. Sponges

8. Which of the following has a true coelom?
    a. Roundworm
    b. Earthworm
    c. Pinworm
    d. Hookworm

9. Klinefelter syndrome occurs in humans who have an extra X chromosome. All of the following are true about Klinefelter syndrome except:
    a. Klinefelter syndrome results when a normal egg is fertilized by sperm containing both the X and Y chromosome.
    b. Klinefelter syndrome results when a normal sperm fertilizes an egg that contains both of its original X and X chromosomes.
    c. The zygote has 46 chromosomes.
    d. Klinefelter syndrome occurs when there is nondisjunction during the formation of egg or sperm.

10. Oxpeckers are a kind of bird often found on the backs of rhinoceros. They pull ticks and other parasites from the rhino's skin and eat them. The oxpecker has a food supply while the rhino has pest control. The relationship between the oxpecker and the rhinoceros is an example of:
    a. Mutualism
    b. Commensalism
    c. Parasitism
    d. Predator-Prey

11. All of the following are products of the dark reaction of photosynthesis, except:
    a. $C_6H_{12}O_6$
    b. ADP
    c. $NADP^+$
    d. ATP

12. If *B* represents a dominant allele and *b* represents the recessive allele, what are the genotypes of parents that produce 30 offspring with the dominant trait and 10 offspring with the recessive trait?
    a. *Bb* x *Bb*
    b. *BB* x *Bb*
    c. *BB* x *BB*
    d. *BB* x *bb*

13. Which of the following represents the end product of the Calvin-Benson cycle?
    a. ADP, CO_2, H_2O
    b. ATP, NADH, $FADH_2$, CO_2
    c. ADP, $NADP^+$, $C_6H_{12}O_6$
    d. NADH, FAD^+, CO_2

14. Which one of the following reproduces through seeds that are contained by fruit?
    a. Pine cone
    b. Angiosperms
    c. Cypress
    d. Gymnosperms

15. If a gene sequence changes from *BCDEFG* to *BCGEFD*, this is an example of:
    a. Frameshift mutation
    b. Deletion
    c. Substitution
    d. Inversion

Additional Biology Practice - Answers

1. B
2. D
3. A
4. D
5. C
6. A
7. C
8. B
9. C
10. A
11. D
12. A
13. C
14. B
15. D

59690929R00054

Made in the USA
Lexington, KY
13 January 2017